Basic Composition for ESL
An Expository Workbook

2ND EDITION

Jann Huizenga
La Guardia Community College, City University of New York

Courtenay Meade Snellings

Gladys Berro Francis
Community College of Allegheny County

Scott, Foresman and Company
Glenview, Illinois
London, England

An Instructor's Manual is available. It may be obtained through a local Scott, Foresman representative or by writing to English Editor, College Division, Scott, Foresman and Company, 1900 E. Lake Avenue, Glenview, IL 60025.

Art by Kim Crowley

Library of Congress Cataloging-in-Publicaton Data

Huizenga, Jann.
  Basic composition for ESL.

  Includes index.
  1. English language—Rhetoric—Problems, exercises, etc. 2. English language—Text books for foreign speakers. I. Meade Snellings, Courtenay. II. Francis, Gladys Berro. III. Title.
PE1413.H85   1986   808′.042   85-26254

Copyright © 1986, 1982, Scott, Foresman and Company.
All Rights Reserved.

Printed in the United States of America.
ISBN 0-673-18208-8

    456-KPF-9190898887

PREFACE

This writing workbook has been designed for university-bound students or professionals who are studying English as a second language at the advanced-beginning or intermediate level (approximate TOEFL range 320-420). It is flexible enough, however, to be used by any others wanting to improve their basic writing skills. Specifically, the text is intended to be used after students have gained rudimentary competence in sentence-level writing. It provides material for about 60 class hours of instruction, or a 12-week writing course.

Basic Composition for ESL is rooted in the belief that basic organizational skills and modes of communication *can* and *should* be taught at a very early stage in the non-native student's writing career; they need not be postponed, as they often have been, until students have a firm grasp of sentence-level grammar. Students who concentrate from the outset on writing as grammar, ignoring writing as organized communication, must often break bad habits in advanced writing courses. Therefore, this text undertakes to develop an *early* approach to writing as coherent, meaningful communication, even though this communication is as yet grammatically simple. Straightforward, step-by-step explanations and exercises guide the student. Six practical and academic writing purposes are covered in six units: *Giving Instructions, Objective Reporting, Analyzing by Cause and Effect, Comparing and Contrasting, Classifying,* and *Describing a Mechanism or a Process.*

It is important that writing assignments offer control at this level, but at the same time, they must provide creative outlets. *Basic Composition for ESL* offers a middle-ground balance of control and creativity. This situation of "controlled creativity" is set up in the first two sections of each unit by a model composition displaying the rhetorical purpose under discussion, followed first by exercises on organization and grammar and then by an outlining/writing assignment that parallels the model composition and for which students receive visual cues. Both the vocabulary and the organizational principles which students need to use are similar to those of the model composition. The structure of the picture outline gives students strict working guidelines. At the same time, however, because of the visual rather than verbal nature of the cues, students feel responsible for generating the sentences. The picture outlines leave room for student creativity and invention; within guidelines, they can try new lexical items and grammatical structures and expand on the topic by adding their own details. For more secure students, this option to take risks is important. By the third section of each unit, the control gives way to looser guidance; students are encouraged to experiment with what they have learned by writing on one of four suggested unillustrated topics, or developing their own topic.

Basic Composition for ESL is structured so that the six writing purposes and the general content of the units gradually increase in complexity. Each unit opens with a brief introduction discussing the writing purpose taught in that unit and pointing out its academic and practical use. There are three sections per unit, and each section contains the following segments: **Model Composition, Organization, Grammar and Punctuation, Student Outline,** and **Student Composition.**

Each *model composition* is a short prose piece illustrating in clear and simple language the form of the rhetorical purpose in question. The topics are diverse and of potential use and interest to foreign students: "How to Make a Good Impression at an American Dinner Party," "The First Manned Flight to the Moon," "Earthquakes," and so on. The *organization* segment requires students actively to work through the writing process. Outlining, logical relationships, main idea sentences, transitions, and paragraph development are introduced here in a simple and structured manner. The *grammar and punctuation* segment treats grammatical structures and punctuation points as they are relevant to the writing purpose in question. Finally, the *student outlines* and *student compositions* provide visual controls in the first two sections of each unit while providing relative freedom in the final section.

This second edition places a new emphasis on writing which is both process-oriented and reader-oriented. In the *Stepping Along* activities in each *student composition* section, students are guided by a series of suggested steps designed to make them aware of process and reader. Group brainstorming, drafting, peer reading, and redrafting are among the suggested activities. The steps are adaptable and may, of course, be used, omitted, or changed, according to student needs and teacher preference. In the *Stepping Along* activities, where students are working on an initial draft, their attention has been drawn primarily to clarity of content and organization. We feel that students should get down the substance of what they want to say before worrying about polishing it. Thus, we have chosen to leave specific editing activities for last and up to the discretion of individual teachers, but for easy reference we have included a chart of correction symbols on the last page of the text which may be used to help students edit their work. This edition also encourages a more active approach to looking at model compositions. In all but initial sections of each unit, model outlines have been left incomplete. Students must analyze the structure of the written text to fill in the missing pieces.

Basic Composition for ESL has several other important features as well. The numerous illustrations throughout enliven the text and can be used effectively to elicit oral production in a pre-outlining/writing phase. Perforated pages let students tear out assignments to hand in. A glossary at the end of the book provides simple definitions and examples of terms used within the text. Finally, the accompanying *Instructor's Manual* provides an answer key for the instructor's convenience, detailed comments on general and specific ways to use the text, discussion of problems that may arise, and suggestions for the correction of student compositions.

We appreciate the helpful input of our students over the past few years which has been of great assistance in the writing of the second edition. We are grateful to Professors Douglas Ewing, Phyllis L. Lim, and David Van Duren for reviewing the entire second edition manuscript and suggesting ways to improve it. We thank them and Professors John Coates, Richard Eisman, Nick Franks, Carol Heard, Marie Hero, Judy W. Saunders, and Tamara Taylor for their constructive response to the revision questionnaire.

We thank our editors Anne Smith, Patricia Rossi, and Jeanne Schwaba. We appreciate their efforts in coordinating the project. Artist Kim Crowley deserves special thanks for his illustrations.

Finally, gratitude is due to our families, whose patience and support are deeply appreciated. We particularly thank our husbands, Kim, Bill, and Vic, for sharing their general and technical knowledge with us.

Jann Huizenga
Courtenay M. Snellings
Gladys B. Francis

CONTENTS

Introduction XIII

    What is a composition?
    What is a paragraph?
    What does a paragraph look like?
    How does a paragraph begin?
    How does a paragraph progress?
    What holds a paragraph together?

Unit One
Giving Instructions 1

    Introduction 1

Model Composition 1
How to Make a Good Impression at an American Dinner Party 2
    Organization 2
        Outlining
        Main idea sentences
        Transitions showing chronological order
    Grammar and Punctuation 6
        The imperative
        Should
        Using *before, after,* and *when* to show order
        Punctuation with items in a series

Student Outline 1
How to Make a Good Impression at a Job Interview 15
Student Composition 1
How to Make a Good Impression at a Job Interview 18

Model Composition 2
How to Use a Copying Machine   20
    Organization   21
        Outlining
        Transitions showing chronological order
        Irrelevant sentences
    Grammar and Punctuation   23
        Using *and* to join two sentences
        Review: using *before* and *after*

Student Outline 2
How to Use a Commercial Washing Machine   26
Student Composition 2
How to Use a Commercial Washing Machine   29

Model Composition 3
How to Get to Arlington National Cemetery from the White House   31
    Organization   31
        Outlining
        Transitions showing chronological order
        Main idea sentences
    Grammar and Punctuation   36
        Showing directions with *go*

Student Outline and Composition 3   40

Unit Two
Telling What Happened:
Objective Reporting   43

    Introduction   43
Model Composition 4
An Automobile Accident   45
    Organization   46
        Outlining
        Chronological order
        Main idea sentences
        Being precise
    Grammar and Punctuation   50
        Punctuation with introductory phrases
        Punctuation with appositives
        Indirect speech

Student Outline 4
A Motorcycle Accident   57

Student Composition 4
A Motorcycle Accident   60

Model Composition 5
The First Manned Flight to the Moon   62
    Organization   63
        Outlining
        Being precise
        Irrelevant sentences
    Grammar and Punctuation   65
        Additional uses of the comma
        Indirect speech

Student Outline 5
The First Non-Stop Solo Transatlantic Flight   70

Student Composition 5
The First Non-Stop Solo Transatlantic Flight   73

Model Composition 6
Independence Day in Middleburg   75
    Organization   76
        Outlining
        Major points and additional details
        Main idea sentences
    Grammar and Punctuation   80
        Capitalization
        Punctuation review

Student Outline and Composition 6   83

Unit Three
Analyzing by Cause and Effect   85

    Introduction   85

Model Composition 7
Why Blake College Is Popular   87
    Organization   88
        Outlining
        Understanding the cause-effect relationship
        Major points and additional details
        Main idea sentences
        Transitions showing addition

Student Outline 7
Why Croft College Is Unpopular   98

Student Composition 7
Why Croft College Is Unpopular   100

Model Composition 8
Why Sandra Miller Is Not Healthy   102
    Organization   103
        Outlining
        Major points and additional details
        The cause-effect relationship
        Irrelevant sentences
    Grammar and Punctuation   107
        Showing cause effect with *because*
        Punctuation with adverbial clauses: summary

Student Outline 8
Why Bob Adams Is Healthy   112

Student Composition 8
Why Bob Adams Is Healthy   115

Model Composition 9
The Causes of Famine   117
    Organization   118
        Outlining
        Major points and additional details
        Main idea sentences
    Grammar and Punctuation   122
        Showing cause-effect with *because of*
        Showing cause-effect with *so* and *therefore*
        Punctuation review

Student Outline and Composition 9   128

Unit Four
Comparing and Contrasting   131

    Introduction   131

Model Composition 10
My Two Brothers   133
    Organization   134
        Outlining
        Main idea sentences
        Introductions

      Finding similarities and differences
      Using *both* for similarities
      Using *but* for differences
      Transitions showing contrast: *on the other hand*
   Grammar and Punctuation   149
      Comparatives

Student Outline 10
Two Sisters   153

Student Composition 10
Two Sisters   157

Model Composition 11
Two Houses for Sale   159
   Organization   161
      Outlining
      Irrelevant sentences
   Grammar and Punctuation   162
      Transitions showing contrast: *however*
      However/but review
      Using *neither* for similarities
      Neither/both review

Student Outline 11
Two Apartments for Rent   171

Student Composition 11
Two Apartments for Rent   174

Model Composition 12
Two Cities   176
   Organization   177
      Outlining
      Transitions showing contrast and similarity
      Main idea sentences and introductions
      Conclusions
   Grammar and Punctuation   185
      Comparing with *as...as*
      Review of comparatives
      Showing contrast with *although*

Student Outline and Composition 12   192

Unit Five
Classifying 195

    Introduction 195

Model Composition 13
Amount of Carbohydrate in Foods 197
    Organization 198
        Outlining
        Classification charts
        More practice with general and specific
        Main idea sentences and introductions
        Transitions for giving examples
    Grammar and Punctuation 208
        Punctuation: the colon

Student Outline 13
Amount of Protein in Foods 210

Student Composition 13
Amount of Protein in Foods 212

Model Composition 14
Contact Sports 214
    Organization 215
        Outlining
        Irrelevant sentences
    Grammar and Punctuation 218
        Passive voice
        Punctuation: review of the colon

Student Outline 14
Noncontact Sports 222

Student Composition 14
Noncontact Sports 225

Model Composition 15
The Uses of Cattle 227
    Organization 228
        Outlining
        Classification charts
        Main idea sentences and introductions
        Conclusions
        Transition review
        Giving examples with *such as*
    Grammar and Punctuation 237
        Punctuation review

Student Outline and Composition 15 238

Unit Six
Describing a Mechanism or a Process   241

Introduction   241
Model Composition 16   A Television   243
Organization   244
Outlining
Main idea sentences and introductions
Identifying the parts of a mechanism
Grammar and Punctuation   250
Relative clauses: nonrestrictive

Student Outline 16   An AM/FM Radio   257

Student Composition 16   An AM/FM Radio   259

Model Composition 17
The Human Respiratory System   261
Organization   262
Outlining
Explaining the operation of a mechanism or process
Irrelevant sentences
Grammar and Punctuation   267
Review: nonrestrictive relative clauses
Relative clauses: restrictive
Relative clauses: omitting the relative pronoun + the form of *to be*

Student Outline 17
The Human Circulatory System   273

Student Composition 17
The Human Circulatory System   275

Model Composition 18   Earthquakes   277
Organization   278
Outlining
Introductions
Conclusions
Grammar and Punctuation   281
Review: relative clauses

Student Outline and Composition 18   285

Glossary   289

Index   295

Correction Symbols   298

INTRODUCTION

The aim of this book is to teach you some basic points about writing. Knowing how to express ideas in writing in an organized way is important for everybody, but it is especially important for you as a student or professional. By the time you finish this book, you will have mastered the basic steps of the writing process and will be able to write compositions for six practical and academic purposes.

What is a composition?

A **composition** is a piece of writing about one central topic. It may consist of one or more paragraphs. If the central topic is broad and needs to be divided into several subtopics, each of these subtopics should be developed in at least one paragraph. For instance, if you want to discuss *types of food,* you may want to break your central topic down into four subtopics: *meat, dairy products, vegetables,* and *grain.* You might use, then, a separate paragraph for each subtopic. A composition of more than one paragraph usually has an introduction and a conclusion which are separate paragraphs.

What is a paragraph?

A **paragraph** is a group of related sentences which communicates one central idea. A paragraph may be short or long according to the simplicity or complexity of the subject.

What does a paragraph look like?

The first line of a paragraph must be indented. This means that you must leave an empty space to show the beginning of the paragraph. A composition that has one paragraph will have only one indentation. A composition that has two paragraphs will have two indentations, and so on. Make sure that you capitalize the first word in each sentence and end each sentence with a period. If your paragraph is a composition, put your title at the top of the page.

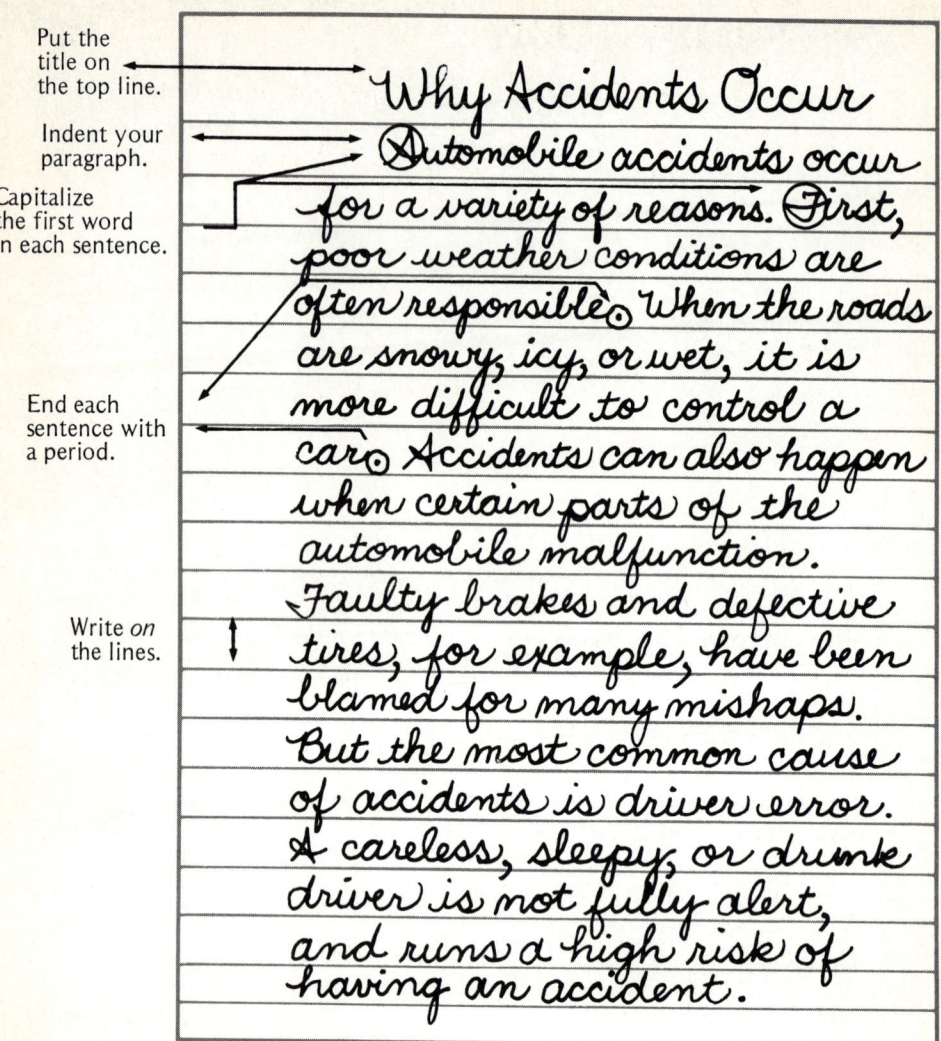

How does a paragraph begin?

A paragraph usually begins with a general statement. We call this general statement the **main idea sentence**, though it is sometimes called a topic sentence. The main idea sentence tells the reader what the paragraph is about and limits the kind of information that should be included in the paragraph. The main idea sentence is usually the first sentence of the paragraph, but experienced writers sometimes place it in the middle or at the end of the paragraph.

How does a paragraph progress?

The main idea sentence is followed by **major points.** The major points are the sentences that explain the main idea sentence. They give more information about it. Below, the major points of the paragraph are in italics. They are expanded with **additional details.**

>   Automobile accidents occur for a variety of reasons. *First, poor weather conditions are often responsible.* When the roads are snowy, icy, or wet, it is more difficult to control a car. *Accidents can also happen when certain parts of the automobile malfunction.* Faulty brakes and defective tires, for example, have been blamed for many mishaps. *But the most common cause of accidents is driver error.* A careless, sleepy, or drunk driver is not fully alert and runs a high risk of having an accident.

What holds a paragraph together?

Ideas in a paragraph are often connected with **transitions.** Transitions show the relationship between these ideas. Transitions include words such as *first, finally, in addition, for example,* and *in contrast.* Without transitions, your paragraph will not read smoothly. You will learn to use different kinds of transitions for different purposes. Transitions are also used between paragraphs.

UNIT ONE
Giving Instructions

INTRODUCTION

In this unit you will practice writing clear instructions. When you give instructions, you explain how to do something. You are giving instructions when you tell someone how to cook a chicken, how to get downtown, or how to change a tire. In academic and professional situations, it is often necessary to explain clearly in writing how to do something. You might need to explain, for example, how to conduct a chemical experiment, how to diagnose a certain illness, or how to program a new computer. There are several important points to remember when you write instructions.

1. *Use chronological order.* First and most importantly, when you tell someone how to do something, remember to write the steps for the process in exact order, just as you do them. If you are explaining how to cook a chicken, for example, you need to tell how to clean it before you tell how to season it.
2. *Keep your audience in mind.* You must decide before you begin to write whom the instructions will be for. A city resident and a tourist will not need the same directions for going downtown.
3. *Be clear.* Explain your instructions clearly. Keep your sentences short. If they are confusing, your reader may not be able to follow your directions correctly.
4. *Be thorough.* Explain each step carefully—not only *what* to do but *how* to do it. For example, when explaining how to change a tire, don't just tell your reader to raise the car. Instead, explain exactly how high to raise it and what tool to use.
5. *Be exact.* Make sure your facts and details are precise. If you are giving directions, say, "Go twelve blocks" instead of, "Go about half a mile."
6. *Stick to the point.* Be sure all the information you include is related to your main purpose. When telling how to change a tire, don't discuss where to buy cheap tires or how long new ones should last. Such details may interest the reader, but they won't help in changing the tire.
7. *Be complete.* Be very careful not to leave out any steps. Remember, you know how to do what you are explaining, but your reader might not.

MODEL COMPOSITION 1
How to Make a Good Impression at an American Dinner Party

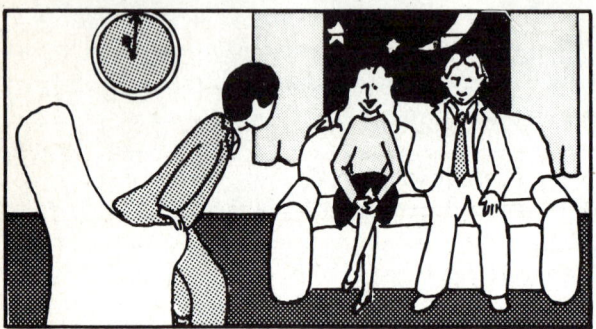

Making a good impression at an American dinner party is not difficult if you follow these instructions. First, you should buy a small gift such as flowers, candy, or wine for your host or hostess. Second, arrive on time. If the dinner engagement is for 7:00, don't arrive after 7:15 without telephoning. Next, during dinner, be sure to compliment your host or hostess on the meal. After you finish eating, you should not stay more than a few hours. Finally, thank your host or hostess for the dinner when you leave.

ORGANIZATION

Outlining

It is often useful to make an **outline** before you begin to write. Your outline will help you organize your thoughts. Begin your outline with a main idea sentence. Then list your **major points**. All these major points relate directly to the main idea sentence. For a short composition which gives instructions, your major points will be steps listed in **chronological order;** you will tell what should be done first, what should be done second, and so on.

Examine this outline of the model composition carefully. You will write your own at the end of this section.

Outline of Model Composition 1

Main idea sentence: Making a good impression at an American dinner party is not difficult if you follow these instructions.

1. Buy a small gift for your host or hostess.
2. Arrive on time.
3. During dinner, be sure to compliment your host or hostess on the meal.
4. Do not stay more than a few hours after the meal.
5. Thank your host or hostess for the dinner when you leave.

Main Idea Sentences

The main idea or main point of a composition is contained in the **main idea sentence.** This sentence tells the reader what you are writing about in general. You should write your main idea sentence at the beginning of your composition. (When you become a more experienced writer, you may learn other techniques.) Your explanation and specific examples will follow. Underline the main idea sentence in the model composition.

A main idea sentence for a composition which gives instruction tells 1) what the instructions will cover, 2) that the necessary steps for this process will follow, and 3) (optional) why the reader might be interested in reading further.

EXAMPLES

Note how the following examples show the above points.

If you want to grow healthy roses, follow these important steps.
 (1)   (2)

A salad is a delicious dinner vegetable, and you can make a good one
 (3)   (1)

by following these directions.
 (2)

4 BASIC COMPOSITION FOR ESL

EXERCISE 1-A

Choose the best main idea sentence for each of the following paragraphs.

1. First, you should call the telephone company. Give the company representative your name and address. Next, explain what kind of service and what kind of phone you want. Send a deposit if you have never had a phone before. Someone at the phone company will then arrange a convenient time to have the phone installed.

   a. Deciding what kind of phone you want is not difficult.
   b. In order to get a phone, follow these directions.
   c. If you want to get a phone for the first time, you need to pay a small deposit.

2. First, crack two eggs into a bowl. Add two tablespoons of milk or water and a little salt and pepper. Beat the mixture well with a fork. Then you should melt a tablespoon of butter in a small frying pan and pour the egg mixture into the pan. Cook it on medium-high heat for five minutes. When the omelet becomes firm on the bottom, lay thin slices of cheese on it. Cook it a minute longer. Then fold it in half with a spatula. Finally, carefully remove the omelet from the pan and serve it.

   a. You need a frying pan and a spatula in order to make a cheese omelet.
   b. I often make cheese omelets in the following way because they are good.
   c. A cheese omelet is delicious for breakfast, lunch, or dinner, and you will have no trouble making one if you follow these steps.

3. First, wrap your package well. Print the receiver's address in the middle of the package and your address in the upper left-hand corner. Then go to the post office. Go up to one of the windows, and give your package to the clerk. You should tell the clerk whether you want it to go first, third, or fourth class (second class is used only for newspapers and periodicals) and if you want to insure it. Finally, pay your money.

   a. If you want to send a package from the U.S., you must go to the post office.
   b. Sending a package from the U.S. is not difficult if you follow these simple instructions.
   c. If you want a package to arrive at its destination fast, send it first class.

Transitions Showing Chronological Order

When you write, you want your reader to follow you easily as you move from one part of your composition to another. We often use **transitions** to help the reader see the relationship between the parts. Transitions can show the relationship between sentences and between paragraphs. When giving instructions, you will want to use transitions which show the *time* relationship between the steps. Some of these transitions are:

First, . . . (Second, Third, etc.)
Next, . . .
Then . . .
Finally/Lastly, . . .

Commas are usually used after all of the above transitions except *then*. Use these words carefully. Too many transitions might make your composition monotonous.

EXERCISE 1-B

1. Below is a main idea sentence followed by four sentences. Place the sentences in proper chronological order by numbering them. (Number 1 has already been indicated.) Then rewrite all sentences in paragraph form, choosing words from the group of transitions. Don't use more than 3 transitions.

   If you need to take a taxi in New York City, follow these steps.

   _____ Tell the driver where you want to go.

   _1_ Step into the street and flag one down.

   _____ Pay and tip the driver upon arrival.

   _____ Get in the back seat.

   _____
   _____
   _____
   _____
   _____
   _____

2. Now do the same with these sentences.

   Travelers' checks are a safe way to carry money when traveling, and you can purchase them in the following manner.

   _____ Ask a teller to give you the desired amount of checks.

   _____ Sign your name once in the appropriate spot on each check before you leave the bank.

_____ Go to your local bank.

_____ Pay your money plus a small service charge.

_____
_____
_____
_____
_____
_____
_____
_____
_____

GRAMMAR AND PUNCTUATION

The Imperative

The **imperative** form of the verb is used to give instructions, to make requests, and to give orders. You will use this form frequently when you write instructions. The imperative consists of the base form of the verb without a **subject pronoun.** To make the imperative negative, put *do not* or *don't* before the verb.

EXAMPLES

Finally, *thank* your host or hostess for the dinner.
Be sure to compliment your host or hostess on the meal.

Don't arrive after 7:15 without telephoning.
After you finish eating, *do not stay* more than a few hours.

Note: Many of the sentences in the outline of Model Composition 1 are imperative.

EXERCISE 1-C

Using the following pictures, imagine you are telling a friend how to take a plane. Use the imperative form.

    Helpful vocabulary: check luggage
                                 board a plane
                                 flight attendant

1. *Find the ticket counter.*

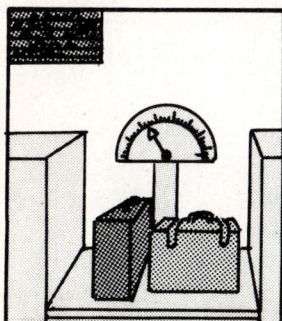

2.

3.

8 BASIC COMPOSITION FOR ESL

 4.

EXERCISE 1-D

Imagine you are telling your friend what *not* to do. Use the following pictures to write negative commands.

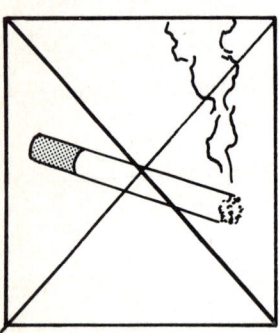 1. *Please don't smoke.*

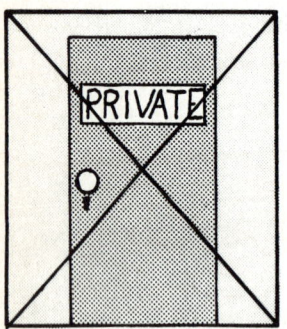 2.

GIVING INSTRUCTIONS 9

3.

4.

5.

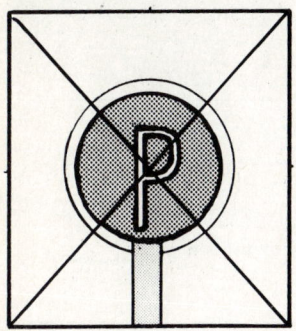
6.

Should

You just learned how to give your reader instructions using the imperative form. You can also use *should* or *should not (shouldn't)* for this purpose. *Should* is followed by the base form of a verb.

EXAMPLES

You should buy a small gift for your host or hostess.

After you finish eating, *you should not stay* more than a few hours.

EXERCISE 1-E

I have several problems. Tell me what I should or shouldn't do in the following situations.

1. I have a bad toothache.

    You should see a dentist right away.
    You shouldn't eat so much candy!

2. I'm gaining too much weight.

    _____
    _____

3. I want to learn Spanish as quickly as possible.

    _____
    _____

4. I'm living far from my family and friends, and I'm very homesick.

    _____
    _____

5. I usually get a headache when I listen to loud music.

_____

_____

6. I'm late to class every morning.

_____

_____

7. I'm having a hard time making new friends in this city.

_____

_____

Using *Before, After* and *When* to Show Order

When we give instructions, we often use dependent clauses beginning with *before, after,* or *when* to show the sequence of steps. A **clause** is a group of words which contains a subject and a verb. There are two kinds of clauses: main clauses and dependent clauses. A **main** clause can be a separate sentence. A **dependent** clause, however, depends on a main clause for its complete meaning and cannot be a sentence by itself. Each of the following sentences contains a main clause and a dependent clause. Underline the dependent clause in each.

Thank your host or hostess for the dinner when you leave.

After you finish eating, do not stay more than a few hours.

Make an appointment before you go to the office.

EXAMPLES

The following examples show you how *before* and *after* are used to combine two imperative clauses. Notice that the subject *(you)* appears in the dependent clause. If the dependent clause comes first, it is separated from the main clause by a comma.

1. Add the rest of the ingredients.
2. Beat the mixture.

After you add the rest of the ingredients, beat the mixture.

Beat the mixture *after* you add the rest of the ingredients.

Before you beat the mixture, add the rest of the ingredients.

Add the rest of the ingredients *before* you beat the mixture.

When indicates that two steps occur at the same time.

When you leave, thank your host or hostess.

Thank your host or hostess *when* you leave.

EXERCISE 1-F

Punctuate the following sentences where necessary.

1. After you check your luggage go directly to the gate.
2. Before the taxi comes make sure you have enough money.
3. Get off the bus after it has come to a complete stop.
4. When you reach your destination pay and tip the taxi driver.
5. Buy your ticket before you board the plane.
6. Before the plane takes off fasten your seat belt.

EXERCISE 1-G

Now combine the sentences with the words in parentheses. Write each sentence two ways.

1. a. Put your books away.
   b. Begin your test.   (before)

Before you begin your test, put your books away.

Put your books away before you begin your test.

2. a. Buy your movie ticket.
   b. Find a seat.   (after)

3. a. Arrive at the exam.
   b. Remain silent.   (when)

4. a. Do stretching exercises.
   b. Begin to jog.   (before)

5. a. Pick up the telephone receiver.
   b. Drop 25¢ in the coin slot.   (after)

Punctuation with Items in a Series

Commas are used to separate items in a series. These items may be words, phrases, or clauses. Do not use a comma if only two items are mentioned.

EXAMPLES

Buy a small gift such as flowers, candy, or wine.

Baseball, football, tennis, and golf are popular sports in the U.S.

She thanked the host and hostess. (no comma needed)

EXERCISE 1-H

Punctuate these sentences correctly. Note that some sentences do not need additional punctuation.

1. You will need matches, newspapers, twigs, and logs to make a good fire.

2. He bought milk and bread.

3. They will take a vacation in June July or August.

4. Mandarin English Russian Spanish and Hindi all have over 200 million speakers.

5. The three most popular natural sites in the U.S. are the Grand Canyon Yellowstone National Park and Niagara Falls.

6. Bring a pen or a sharp pencil to the test.

7. Eggs celery onions and mayonnaise are the ingredients you will need to make a good egg salad.

8. The hikers took canned food a small tent and sleeping bags on their hike.

9. She hopes to visit the Middle East South America or Australia next year.

STUDENT OUTLINE 1
How to Make a Good Impression at a Job Interview

Imagine that a friend is job hunting and you want to give this friend advice on how to make a good impression at a job interview. The following pictures show you some of the steps which are necessary to make a favorable impression. Use them to write an outline and a main idea sentence. For each picture, write at least one sentence. Use the imperative for most of your sentences. Write one or two sentences using *should*. Use the outline of Model Composition if you need a guide.

    Helpful vocabulary: library
                                  learn about/investigate
                                  wear
                                  interviewer
                                  be polite/be courteous
                                  answer in detail
                                  show interest in

Main idea sentence:* _____

_____

_____

_____

_____

* You may want to write your main idea sentence last.

1.

16 *BASIC COMPOSITION FOR ESL*

2.

3.

4.

GIVING INSTRUCTIONS 17

5.

6.

STUDENT COMPOSITION 1
How to Make a Good Impression at a Job Interview

Stepping Along

Step 1: Use your main idea sentence and your outline to help you write a one-paragraph composition. Use appropriate transitions. Look back at Model Composition 1 or the exercises if you need extra help.

Step 2: Exchange your paragraph with a partner. As you read your partner's composition, think about these questions.
-Is everything in your partner's instructions clear to you?
-Did your partner indent the paragraph?
-Does your partner use good transitions with correct punctuation?
-Can you give your partner any suggestions for improvement?

Step 3: Talk with your partner about your paragraphs. Try to agree on improvements which you can make.

Step 4: Rewrite your composition, making any changes you feel are necessary.

Further steps: As directed by your teacher.

MODEL COMPOSITION 2
How to Use a Copying Machine

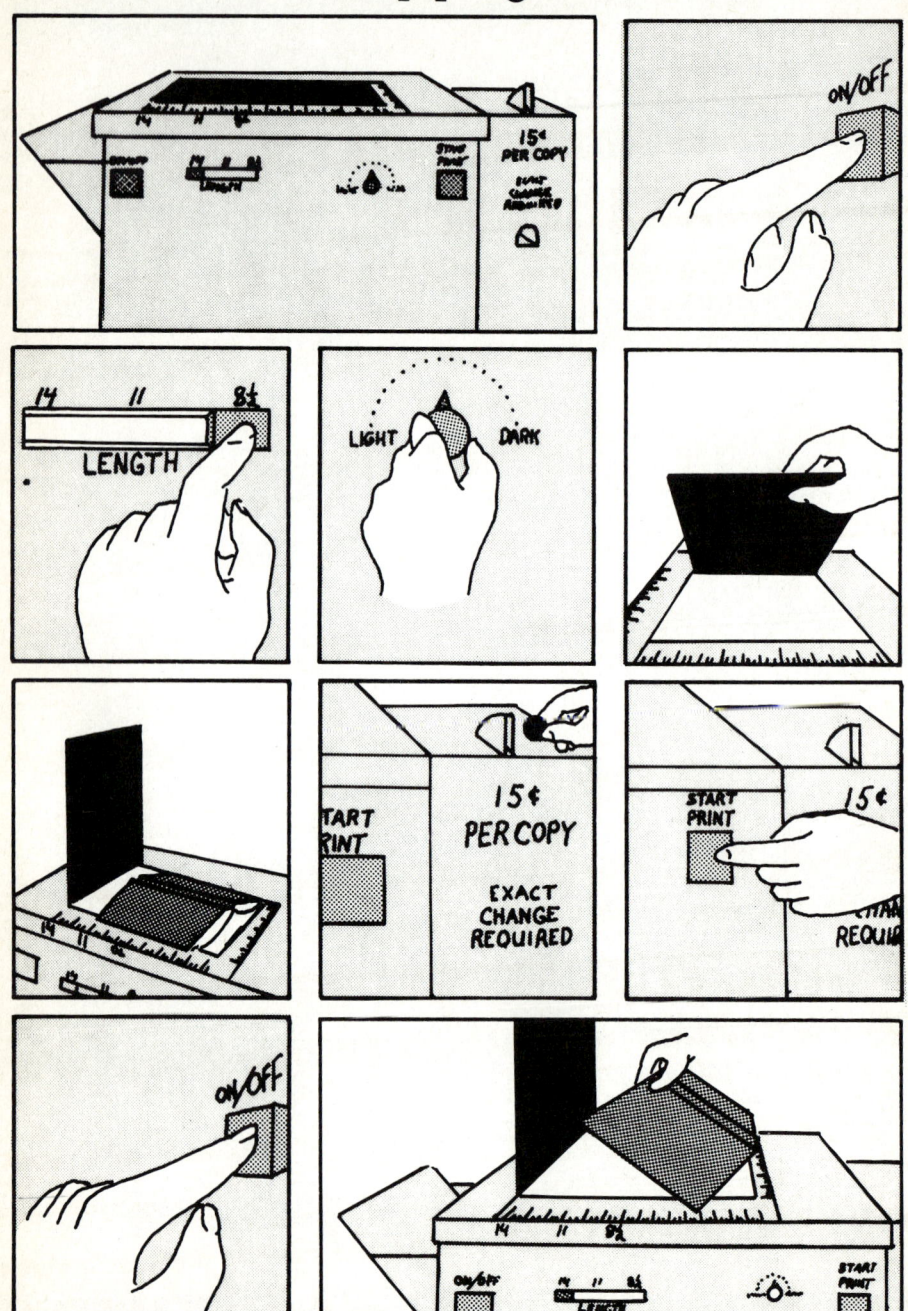

Most copying machines work in a similar way, and they are easy to use if you do the following things. First, you should find out the cost of each copy and get your money ready. Then turn on the machine. Set the page-length control and the light/dark control. Next, lift the cover and place your book or paper face down on the glass. Put your money in the coin slot. Then press the "start print" button. After your copy comes out in the copy tray, turn off the machine. Finally, don't forget to lift the cover and remove your book or paper.

ORGANIZATION

Outlining

Examine the following incomplete outline of the model composition. Can you complete it?

Outline of Model Composition 2

Main idea sentence. Most copying machines work in a similar way, and they are easy to use if you do the following things.

    1. Find out the cost of each copy and get your money ready.

    2. _____

    _____

    3. Set the page-length control.
    4. Set the light/dark control.

    5. _____

    _____

    6. Place your book or paper face down on the glass.

    7. _____

    _____

    8. Press the "start print" button.
    9. Turn off the machine.
    10. Lift the cover, and remove your book or paper.

22 BASIC COMPOSITION FOR ESL

EXERCISE 2-A Transitions Showing Chronological Order

Circle the transitions in Model Composition 2. Is a transition used at the beginning of each sentence? Why not?

Irrelevant Sentences

A main idea sentence is a general statement which immediately tells the reader the topic or subject of the composition. All other sentences in the composition should support or directly relate to the main idea sentence. A sentence is **irrelevant** if it does not directly relate to the main idea sentence. Below is a paragraph containing an irrelevant sentence. It has been crossed out.

EXAMPLE

Fresh orange juice tastes better than frozen orange juice, and it can be made in the following way. First, buy some very fresh oranges. ~~Oranges are grown in areas with warm climates.~~ Next, cut the oranges in half. Squeeze the halves in a juicer until all the juice is out. Then throw away the seeds and the pulp. Finally, add a little sugar if you wish, and drink.

EXERCISE 2-B

In each of the following short compositions, one sentence does not relate to the main idea sentence. Find this irrelevant sentence and cross it out.

1. Following these simple rules may help you find an apartment in a new city. First, if you have friends in the area, ask them if they know of any vacant apartments. If you don't know anyone in the area, look in the classified ads in the newspaper under "Apartments for Rent." You can also find job announcements and cars for sale in the classified ads. Then make phone calls to the apartments that look good to you. If you have no success, look in the phone book under "Real Estate." Call as many real estate offices as you can, and ask if they have any apartments available. Finally, after you get a list of rentals from these offices, go to see the apartments and choose the one you like.

2. You can treat first- and second-degree burns yourself by following these simple instructions. First, immerse the burn in cold water. Remove it when the pain subsides. Next, dry the burn gently with a sterile gauze or a clean cloth. Do not put any pressure on it. When the burn is completely dry, cover it loosely with a dry bandage. Then, if an arm or a leg is burned, raise it higher than the heart. Finally, call a doctor if necessary. Remember that burns often result from carelessness.

3.   Cooking hamburgers outdoors is not difficult if you follow these directions. First, put charcoal on an outdoor grill. Wet the charcoal thoroughly with lighter fluid. Next, light a match and ignite the coals. After starting the fire, wait about thirty minutes until the coals begin to turn gray. Then put the raw hamburger patties on the grill. Sprinkle them with salt and pepper. You should also sprinkle steak, chicken, and pork chops with salt and pepper when you grill them. Turn the hamburgers over after about ten minutes. Cook them for another ten minutes and eat immediately.

GRAMMAR AND PUNCTUATION

Using *And* to Join Two Sentences

Two independent clauses which are related may be joined with *and*. A comma comes before *and* unless the clauses are very short.

EXAMPLE

Most copying machines work in a similar way, *and* they are easy to use if you do the following things.

EXERCISE 2-C

Join the sentences using *and*. Punctuate correctly.

1. First put the charcoal on the grill. Then wet it with lighter fluid.

First, put the charcoal on the grill, and then wet it with lighter fluid.

2. Go to your local bank. Ask a teller to give you the desired amount of checks.

3. Tacos can be made inexpensively. They can also be prepared easily.

4. Place the paper face down on the glass. Put your money in the coin slot.

5. Cut fresh oranges in half. Squeeze them in a juicer until all the juice is out.

EXERCISE 2-D Review: Using *Before* and *After*

Combine the following sentences two ways using the word in parentheses. Omit *then* when you rewrite the sentences.

1. Set the page-length control. Then set the light/dark control.   (after)

After you set the page-length control, set the light/dark control.

Set the light/dark control after you set the page-length control.

2. Turn on the machine. Then set the page-length control.   (before)

3. Place the book or paper face down on the glass. Then put your money in the coin slot.   (after)

4. Lift the cover. Then remove your book or paper.   (before)

5. Set the light/dark control. Then lift the cover.   (after)

STUDENT OUTLINE 2
How to Use a Commercial Washing Machine

Imagine that someone you know has left home to go to college and must use a laundromat for the first time. Use the following pictures to write an outline and a main idea sentence for a set of instructions on how to use a commercial washing machine. Write at least one sentence using the imperative or *should* for each picture. Use the outline of Model Composition 2 if you need a guide.

Helpful vocabulary: load
lid
measure
pour into/add
water-temperature control
fabric selection control
laundry

Main idea sentence: _____

_____

_____

_____

_____

1.

GIVING INSTRUCTIONS   27

2.

3.

4.

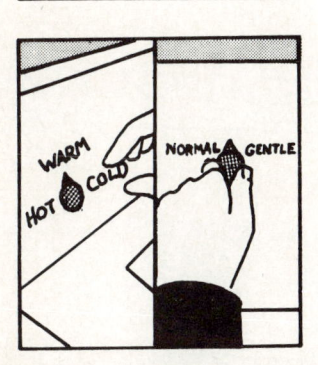

5.

28 BASIC COMPOSITION FOR ESL

6.

7.

8.

STUDENT COMPOSITION 2
How to Use a Commercial Washing Machine

Stepping Along

Step 1: Use your main idea sentence and your outline to help you write a one-paragraph composition. Use *before* and *after* once each, as well as other appropriate transitions. Look back at the model composition or the exercises if you need help.

Step 2: Exchange your composition with a partner. As you read your partner's composition, think about these questions:
-Suppose that you had never used a commercial washing machine. Would you be able to operate one with your partner's instructions?
-Has your partner omitted any steps?
-Are all the instructions clear?
-Are transitions used correctly?
-Can you give your partner suggestions for improvement?

Step 3: Talk with your partner about your paragraphs. Try to agree on improvements which you can make.

Step 4: Rewrite your composition, making any changes you feel are necessary.

Further steps: As directed by your teacher.

MODEL COMPOSITION 3
How to Get to Arlington National Cemetery from the White House

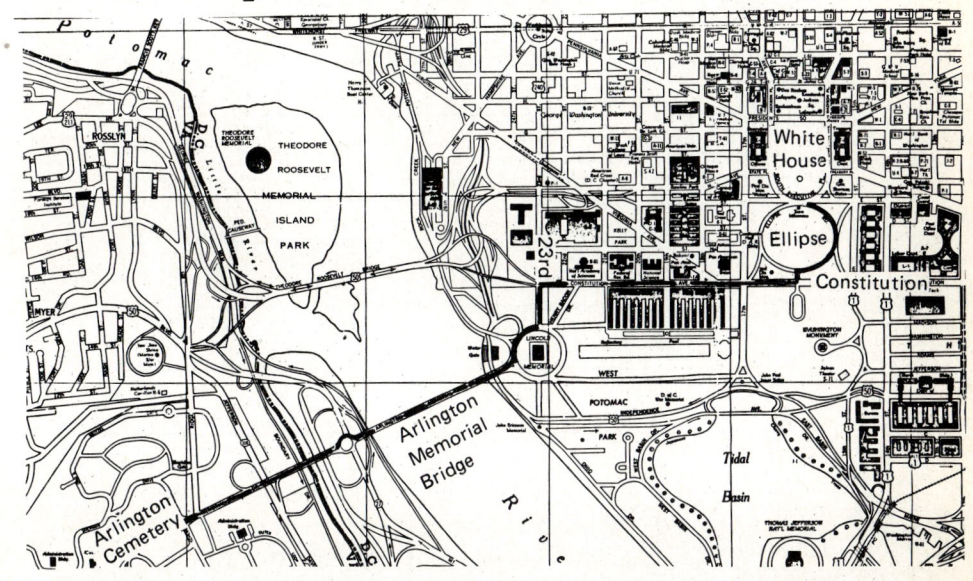

If you are in Washington, D.C., and you want to go from the White House to Arlington National Cemetery, follow these directions and you can get there in eight to ten minutes. First, you should find the Zero Milestone on The Ellipse road across from the White House south lawn. After that, drive halfway around The Ellipse, and turn left on the short access road to Constitution Avenue. You will see the Washington Monument in front of you. Then go right at Constitution Avenue. Drive west along Constitution Avenue to 23rd Street. Turn left and continue along 23rd Street until you enter the traffic circle around the Lincoln Memorial. Take the exit ramp to Arlington Memorial Bridge. This bridge takes you over the Potomac River. At the end of the bridge, there is another traffic circle. Bear right, but do not take any of the exit ramps to the George Washington Memorial Parkway. Continue halfway around the circle, and take the exit road to Arlington National Cemetery. The cemetery will be a half mile down this road.

ORGANIZATION

Outlining

Examine the following incomplete outline of the Model Composition. Can you complete it?

Outline of Model Composition 3

Main idea sentence. If you are in Washington D.C., and you want to go from the White House to Arlington National Cemetery, follow these directions and you can get there in eight to ten minutes.

1. Find the Zero Milestone on The Ellipse road.
2. _____
   _____
3. _____
   _____
4. _____
   _____
5. Drive west along Constitution Avenue to 23rd Street.
6. Turn left on 23rd Street.
7. Enter the traffic circle around the Lincoln Memorial.
8. _____
   _____
9. Bear right at the end of the bridge around another traffic circle.
10. Take the exit road to Arlington National Cemetery.
11. Go a half mile down this road.

Transitions Showing Chronological Order

The transition *after that* (found in Model Composition 3) is used in the same way as *next* and *then*—to show that one event follows another. None of these words is used to connect two sentences.

Check your luggage. { *After that,* / *Next,* / *Then* } go to the gate.

After and *before*, however, are used to connect two sentences.

After you check your luggage, go to the gate.
Before you go to the gate, check your luggage.

EXERCISE 3-A

Using the word in parentheses, rewrite the following sentences to show clearly the time relationship between them.

1. a. Go over the bridge.   (after that)
   b. Bear right onto Green Street.

   _____
   _____

2. a. Turn left onto Green Street.   (after)
   b. Drive a half block to Garden Vista Apartments.

   _____
   _____
   _____

3. a. Drive halfway around the traffic circle.   (then)
   b. Go right at Virginia Avenue.

   _____
   _____
   _____

4. a. Turn right onto Park Street.   (next)
   b. Drive a half mile to King's Highway.

   _____
   _____
   _____

5. a. Go over the bridge.   (before)
   b. Start looking for the exit ramp to Arlington National Cemetery.

   _____

   _____

   _____

6. a. Walk north along River Drive for seven blocks.   (after that)
   b. Look for Oakwood Manor on your left.

   _____

   _____

   _____

EXERCISE 3-B Main Idea Sentences

Write main idea sentences for the paragraphs below.

1. _____

   _____

   _____

   _____

First, put crumpled pieces of newspaper in the fireplace. Lay twigs or small pieces of wood on top of the newspaper. Then put two or three logs on top. Finally, light the newspaper with a match, and you will soon have a beautiful fire.

2. _____

   _____

   _____

   _____

First, find a bucket or a large bowl and a sponge. Fill the bucket with water and add about a cup of ammonia. Then wet the sponge and wipe the window clean. Finally, dry it well with a paper towel. Your window will shine.

3. _____

_____

_____

_____

First, take the cap off the gas tank. Then turn the lever on the gas pump to ON. Put the nozzle in the tank. When you have the amount of gas you want, return the nozzle to the pump. Turn the lever to OFF before paying the attendant.

GRAMMAR AND PUNCTUATION

Showing Directions with *Go*

There are many **prepositions** and **adverbials** that can follow the verb *go*. Some of them are explained by the following diagrams.

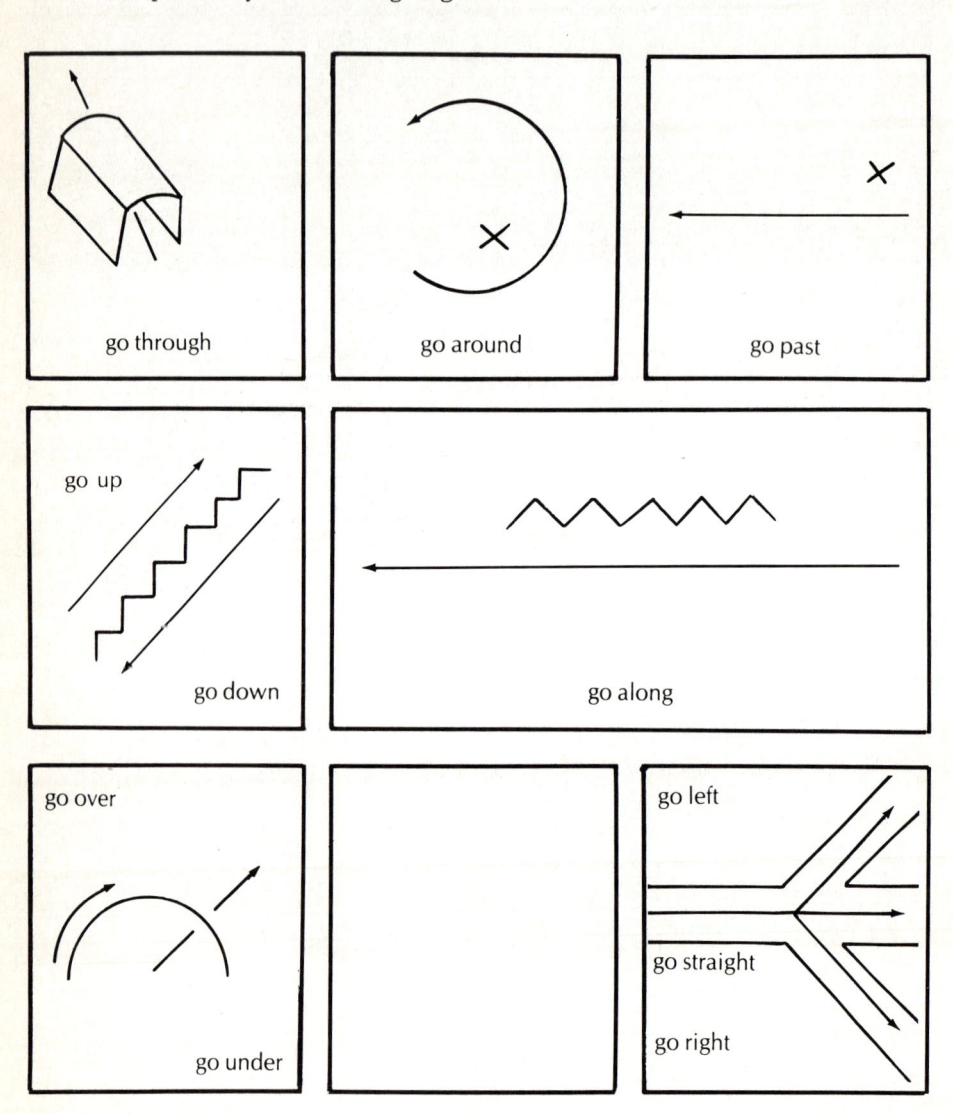

go through

go around

go past

go up

go down

go along

go over

go under

go left

go straight

go right

EXERCISE 3-C

Tell your friend how to find the Admissions Office in this imaginary campus. Write an imperative sentence with *go* for each arrow. Put your instructions in chronological order.

1. *Go through the main entrance.*

2.

3.

4.

5.

6.

EXERCISE 3-D Punctuation Review

Punctuate the following sentences correctly by adding commas. Some need no punctuation.

1. After you finish the experiment put away the chemicals.

2. New York Los Angeles and Chicago are the three largest cities in the United States.

3. Second lay out all necessary materials.

4. Make reservations before you go to a popular restaurant on a Saturday night.

5. The English words *silk tea catsup* and *tycoon* originally come from Chinese.

6. Be sure to thank your host or hostess when you leave.

7. Next add a cup of buttermilk or sour cream to the mixture.

8. Before you come to the exam get a good night's rest.

9. When the mail arrives open it if you wish.

10. You can buy money orders and travelers' cheques at your local bank.

STUDENT OUTLINE AND COMPOSITION 3

Develop your own topic, or choose one of the topics below for a final composition which gives instructions.

1. Imagine that a friend is visiting you from out of town and that she has to drive somewhere. Tell her, for example, how to get to a specific theater or to the airport from your home.
2. Imagine that you are having a party and that you invited your classmate. Tell him how to get to your apartment from the university or college.
3. Explain to your teacher how to make a favorite drink or food from your country (Turkish coffee, Chinese chicken, etc.). Your teacher will probably want to try your recipe, so make your instructions very clear! Be very specific about amount of ingredients and length of cooking time.
4. *CHALLENGER:* Imagine that a friend of yours who knows very little English has just arrived in the United States. Your friend wants to learn English as quickly as possible, but s/he doesn't know where to begin and how to proceed. Tell your friend what you think s/he should do first, second, third, and so on.

Stepping Along

Step 1: After choosing your topic, work in pairs and take turns giving your instructions to each other orally. Ask questions of each other when something is not clear. Remember that you are helping your partner by asking him or her to be specific.

Step 2: On your own, make an outline with a main idea sentence. Be complete and put your steps in chronological order.

Step 3: Exchange your outlines with the same partner. Can you follow your partner's instructions? Has your partner omitted any steps? Discuss your outlines together.

Step 4: Write your instructions in paragraph form. Use appropriate transitions (*first, next,* etc.) and punctuate correctly.

Step 5: Exchange compositions with a new partner. As you read your partner's composition, think about these questions:
-What do you like best about the composition?
-Are all the instructions clear?
-Are transitions used correctly?
-Is the punctuation correct?
-Can you give your partner any suggestions for improvement?

Step 6: Talk with your partner about the strong and weak points of your compositions. Try to agree on improvements which you can make.

Step 7: Rewrite your composition, making any changes you feel are necessary.

Further steps: As directed by your teacher.

UNIT TWO
Telling What Happened: Objective Reporting

INTRODUCTION

In this unit you will learn how to write an **objective report.** An **objective report** is an organized presentation of facts. Its purpose is to tell someone about something that happened. There are many different types of reports, and they are used in many different situations. When we read the newspaper, for instance, we read reports of accidents, fires, and political events. When the sports newscaster on television tells us what happened in the baseball game between the Philadelphia Phillies and the New York Mets, the newscaster is reporting. When you tell your fellow students what occurred at the foreign student meeting you attended, you are reporting. You will write good objective reports if you remember the following.

1. *Follow chronological order.* You have already learned to follow chronological order when you give instructions. When you write a report, you should follow this same order; tell what happened first, what happened next, and so on.
2. *Be precise.* Being precise means being *exact.* You should give exact information: exact names, times, and places. For instance, when writing a report on a chemical experiment in the laboratory, you should not say, "I filled a test tube half full with water and added a little sugar," but rather, "I filled a test tube half full with water and added three grams of sugar." In a report on the history of Ghana, you should not say, "Ghana became a republic sometime in 1960," but, "Ghana became a republic on July 1, 1960."

3. *Be objective.* Being objective means keeping your opinion out of the report. Because the purpose of a report is to tell what happened, it should not include your own feelings about the events. For instance, when writing a report on an accident in a nuclear power plant, you should not say, "This accident proves that all nuclear power plants should be closed." This might be your point of view, but it should not be included in the factual account of the accident.
4. *Be accurate.* Being accurate means that all dates, numbers, names, and other information in the report must be correct. For example, if you are writing a report on the life of John F. Kennedy, but you are not sure of his birthdate, you should check your information in a reliable sourcebook.

The ability to write good reports will be useful to you as students and professionals. As a history student, for instance, you might be asked to report on the events surrounding the signing of the United Nations Charter in 1945. As a business executive, you might want to report on what happened during an important company meeting. Or, as an engineer, you might need to write a report telling what occurred during the construction of a hydroelectric power plant. These kinds of reports are more sophisticated than those which you will write in this unit, but the same principles apply.

MODEL COMPOSITION 4
An Automobile Accident

On December 28, Mary Chan, town council member, had an automobile accident near the corner of Main Street and Lincoln Avenue. At 10:00 A.M., she was driving down Main Street with a passenger, Jane Fields. It was snowing. At Lincoln Avenue, she turned right. Her car suddenly skidded on a patch of ice. First, she hit another car. Then she hit a tree. Moments later, the police arrived. Both Mary Chan and her passenger reported that they were not injured, but the driver of the other car, Joseph Schwartz, told police that his neck hurt. The police took Mr. Schwartz to Fairfield General Hospital for examination. Ms. Chan's car was damaged, but she and Ms. Fields were able to drive home.

ORGANIZATION

Outlining

This composition is a report similar to one which might appear in a small town newspaper. The writer is writing for a particular *audience* or reader: the citizens of the town. We know this because the name of the town where the accident occurred is not mentioned. The writer assumes that the streets, the hospital, and the town council mentioned in the report are familiar to the readers. What kind of information a writer gives, then, depends on who the audience is. Be sure to remember your reader when you write. During this course, your reader will be your teacher and/or your fellow students, unless you are told otherwise.

Below is the outline of the model composition with the major points arranged in chronological order.

Outline of Model Composition 4

Main idea sentence. On December 28, Mary Chan, town council member, had an automobile accident near the corner of Main Street and Lincoln Avenue.

1. At 10:00 A.M., Mary Chan was driving down Main Street in the snow.
2. She turned right at Lincoln Avenue and skidded on a patch of ice.
3. She hit a car.
4. She hit a tree.
5. The police arrived.
6. The people involved in the accident reported how they felt.
7. The police took Mr. Schwartz to the hospital.
8. Ms. Chan and her passenger drove home.

Chronological Order

When you are reporting, your information should be arranged in chronological order: you should tell what happened first, what happened next, and so on.

OBJECTIVE REPORTING   47

EXERCISE 4-A

The following sentences tell about a fire, but they are not in chronological order. Number them in proper order.

_____   1. Five firefighters arrived at the scene at 5:07 A.M.

_____   2. They fought the blaze for half an hour.

_____   3. Police reported that the fire caused $8000 worth of damage.

__1__   4. The fire at the Cambridge Apartments was first noticed at 5:00 A.M. by Mr. Carl Sims, who called the fire department.

_____   5. They then broke the windows and brought their hoses in.

_____   6. The firefighters immediately awakened and evacuated all residents of the apartment building.

Main Idea Sentences

A main idea sentence for a report should tell the reader 1) *what* particular event is being reported, 2) *who or what* was involved, 3) *where* the event happened, and 4) *when* it happened.

EXAMPLES

Read the following examples of main idea sentences for reports. Does each sentence contain the necessary information for a good main idea sentence?

Three thousand runners participated in the annual Great Race which was held in Pittsburgh on June 2.

On October 16, 1934, Mao Tse-tung and his Red Army began their Long March near Fukein, China.

Carnegie-Mellon University held its homecoming on Saturday, October 13, on the campus.

William Lee of 318 Linden Street was seriously injured in an automobile accident on Route 81 early Monday morning.

EXERCISE 4-B

Read the following reports. Choose the best main idea sentence for each.

1. At 8:00 A.M., the cyclists began to gather at the starting line in Gateway Park. The race began at 9:00 A.M. The cyclists rode down Ardmore Boulevard through the park and on to Ellisville, which is forty miles (64 kilometers) south of Wilton. At 10:41 A.M., the first cyclist, Virginia Lipsky, crossed the finish line and was awarded the $100 first-place prize.
   a. Virginia Lipsky won the first-place prize last Monday.
   b. Seventy cyclists rode through Gateway Park on October 10.
   c. On October 10, seventy cyclists participated in the Schwinn Bicycle Race in Wilton, Oregon.

2. At 1:00 A.M., Mr. Lopez was sleeping upstairs when he heard noises downstairs. He went downstairs and saw two masked men going out the front door with his television set. He waited until they had left, and then he called the police. They arrived at 1:20 A.M. Mr. Lopez gave them a description of the two men and filled out a crime report. The criminals have not yet been caught.
   a. Last Monday evening, two men robbed the home of Juan Lopez of Kentwood Avenue.
   b. Two men took Juan Lopez' television set.
   c. Last Monday evening, the police arrived at Juan Lopez' home at 1:20 A.M.

3. The Louvre was closed to the public on that particular day, and Perruggia, a Louvre employee, simply cut the famous painting from its frame and walked out of the museum. He took it to his home in Paris and hid it in a trunk for two years. In 1913, Perruggia tried to sell the painting to Italy, his native country, for $95,000. He was immediately arrested by Italian officials. The *Mona Lisa* was returned unharmed to France.
   a. On August 21, 1911, Vincenzo Perruggia stole a painting from the Louvre.
   b. The *Mona Lisa,* one of the most famous paintings in the world, was painted in 1506 by Leonardo Da Vinci and hangs in the Louvre.
   c. On August 21, 1911, Vincenzo Perruggia stole the *Mona Lisa* from the Louvre.

Being Precise

When you write an objective report, it is necessary to be *precise.* You must give *exact* details: exact times, names, places, and numbers. For instance, when writing a report about an automobile accident, you should not say, "A few pedestrians were injured," but rather, "Four pedestrians were injured." When you are reporting on a fire, it is more exact to write, "The fire started at 9:00 A.M." than, "The fire occurred in the morning."

OBJECTIVE REPORTING   49

EXERCISE 4-C

Each of the following sentences contains some imprecise information. Underline this imprecise information. Then rewrite each sentence to make it more exact.

1. The winner of the Great Race was *a woman*.

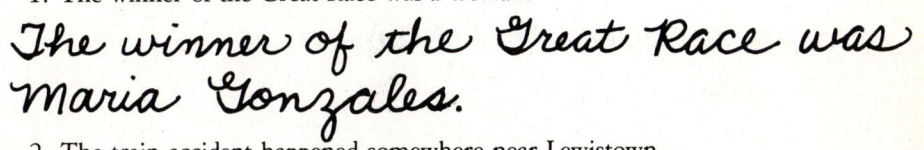

The winner of the Great Race was Maria Gonzales.

2. The train accident happened somewhere near Lewistown.

3. Many people were killed in the crash of Flight 19.

4. Thomas McBain was arrested near his home.

5. Some fire fighters were overcome by smoke.

6. Vesna Moore lost control of her car and hit someone.

7. The final World Series baseball game took place sometime last week.

8. Some people were injured in the chemical explosion in Fabbozzi's factory.

9. There was a serious car accident on a highway in Chicago last night at 8:00 P.M.

10. Some trucks overturned on Route 8.

GRAMMAR AND PUNCTUATION

Punctuation with Introductory Phrases

Several sentences in Model Composition 4 begin with introductory phrases. A **phrase** is a grammatical unit of two or more words without a verb. When a phrase occurs before the main clause, it is called an **introductory** phrase. An introductory phrase, like an introductory clause, is usually followed by a comma. The comma usually separates the introductory phrase from the subject of the sentence. Notice that when the phrase is at the end of the sentence, it requires no punctuation.

EXAMPLES

At Lincoln Avenue, she turned left.

Moments later, the police arrived.

      BUT

She turned left *at Lincoln Avenue.*

The police arrived *moments later.*

OBJECTIVE REPORTING 51

EXERCISE 4-D

Underline all the examples of introductory phrases in the model composition.

EXERCISE 4-E

Decide if the following sentences begin with introductory phrases. If so, put a comma where necessary.

1. Near the post office, John Slovak lost control of his automobile.
2. At the age of twenty-six Albert Einstein published his theory of relativity.
3. The police arrived at the scene of the accident moments after it happened.
4. Color television was first introduced in the U.S. in 1951.
5. In the town of Belleview the express train ran off the track.
6. At the end of World War II representatives from fifty nations helped write the United Nations Charter.
7. It was snowing hard when he hit the parked car.
8. Right in front of her home on Elm Avenue Jeannette Lupis slipped on the ice and broke her leg.
9. From 1920 to 1933 James Joyce's *Ulysses* was banned in the U.S.
10. At the corner of Forbes Avenue and Waverly Drive the crowded bus hit a telephone pole.
11. Every four years athletes from around the world meet and compete in the Olympic Games.
12. The construction of the Taj Mahal started in 1632 and was finished twenty years later.
13. Back in the 1600s many doctors urged patients to smoke because they believed smoking could cure diseases.

14. The Christmas tree originated in Germany in the Middle Ages.

15. On an average weekday more than four million passengers use the New York City subway system.

Punctuation with Appositives

A noun or a noun phrase which immediately follows another noun is called an **appositive**. An appositive explains or defines the noun it follows and is generally set off by commas. Below are examples from the model composition.

EXAMPLES

Mary Chan, *town council member*, had an automobile accident.

(Mary Chan = town council member)

She was driving down Main Street with a passenger, *Jane Fields*.

(passenger = Jane Fields)

The driver of the other car, *Joseph Schwartz*, told police that his neck hurt.

(the driver of the other car = Joseph Schwartz)

EXERCISE 4-F

Decide if these sentences contain appositives. If so, underline the appositives and set them off with commas.

1. The pedestrian , <u>Ivan Popovich</u> , was not seriously injured.

2. The vaccine for rabies was discovered in 1885 by Louis Pasteur a French scientist.

3. The car a 1979 Toyota was badly damaged.

4. Route 401 a major highway through Clayton was very icy last Friday night.

5. The fire at 313 Sheradon Drive caused a great deal of damage.

6. Margaret Mead the famous anthropologist died in 1979 at the age of eighty.

7. Sarah Lloyd's father a passenger in the taxi was not injured in the accident.

OBJECTIVE REPORTING

8. An explosion occurred in the chemical factory in Millvale.

9. The truck avoided hitting the parked car a 1980 Ford.

10. Abraham Lincoln the sixteenth president of the United States is a national hero.

11. Atari a toy and game manufacturer came out with *Pong* the first video screen game in 1972.

12. On Venus the closest planet to the earth there is no water and thus no life.

13. The riot started in a small town called Perth.

14. William Roentgen the discoverer of X-rays received the Nobel Prize in physics in 1901.

15. The Library of Congress in Washington is the largest library in the world.

Indirect Speech

When we wish to report what someone else has said, we often change the speaker's exact words from **direct speech** to **indirect speech**. Indirect speech is frequently used in reports.

When changing from direct to indirect speech,

1. use the **past tense** of the verb if the statement was originally made in the **present tense**
2. insert *that* (optional) when reporting a statement
3. change pronouns where necessary
4. drop the quotation marks.

EXAMPLES

Direct Speech: Ali Luzeri said, "I *feel* fine."
Indirect Speech: Ali Luzeri reported (that) he *felt* fine.

Direct Speech: Leslie Hoffman said, "I *think* my car *is* badly damaged."
Indirect Speech: Leslie Hoffman said (that) she *thought* her car *was* badly damaged.

Direct Speech: The police officer told the woman, "I *want* to see your license."
Indirect Speech: The police officer told the woman (that) he *wanted* to see her license.

The following verbs are used to introduce reported statements: *tell, say, report,* and *announce*. *Report* and *announce* are used when something is said formally, such as in a newspaper or at a formal gathering. Notice that *tell* must always be followed by an indirect object:

She told *someone* that . . .
She said that . . .
He reported that . . .
He announced that . . .

EXERCISE 4-G

The following statements were made at the scene of an automobile accident. Change all the statements to indirect speech.

1. *The driver at fault, Mr. Manning, said that the road was very slippery.*

2.

OBJECTIVE REPORTING **55**

3.

[Panel: "MY NECK HURTS" — MR. MANNING]

4.

[Panel: "YOU'RE LUCKY TO BE ALIVE" — A WITNESS, DR. ANN LAVALLE / MR. AND MRS. MANNING]

5.

[Panel: "MY CAR DOESN'T RUN" — OFFICER MAKOID / MRS. GEORGE, THE DRIVER OF THE OTHER CAR]

6. [Mr. Manning and Mrs. George] "YOU'RE A VERY CARELESS DRIVER"

7. [Mr. Manning] "I REFUSE TO TAKE RESPONSIBILITY"

8. [Officer Makoid and Mr. Manning] "YOU ARE DEFINITELY AT FAULT"

STUDENT OUTLINE 4
A Motorcycle Accident

Imagine that you are a reporter for the school newspaper. A fellow student, Jim Parks, had an accident near school, and you are reporting on it. Use the following pictures to guide you in writing an outline and a main idea sentence for the report. Make your information detailed and precise. Use the outline of Model Composition 4 as a guide.

    Helpful vocabulary: skid on wet pavement
                                    sidewalk
                                    pedestrians
                                    knock over
                                    dented (car or motorcycle)

Main idea sentence: _____

_____

_____

_____

1.

58 BASIC COMPOSITION FOR ESL

2.

3.

4.

5.

OBJECTIVE REPORTING   **59**

6.

7.

8.

STUDENT COMPOSITION 4
A Motorcycle Accident

Stepping Along

Step 1: Write a one-paragraph report using your main idea sentence, your outline, at least one introductory phrase, and appositives to identify each person who was involved in the accident. Be precise.

Step 2: Exchange your composition with a partner. As you read your partner's report, think about these questions:
-Do you get a clear picture of the accident from this report?
-Has your partner included all important details?
-Can you give your partner any suggestions for improvement?

Step 3: Talk with your partner about your compositions and try to agree on improvements you can make.

Step 4: Rewrite your composition, making any changes you feel are necessary.

Further steps: As directed by your teacher.

MODEL COMPOSITION 5
The First Manned Flight to the Moon

OBJECTIVE REPORTING   63

The first manned flight to the moon began when Apollo 11 blasted off from Cape Kennedy, Florida, at 9:32 A.M. on July 16, 1969, with Armstrong, Aldrin, and Collins as the astronauts. Four days after the blast-off, Armstrong and Aldrin moved from the command module, *Columbia,* into the lunar module, *Eagle,* and the two modules separated. Collins continued to orbit the moon in the command module, while the other astronauts descended toward the moon. At 4:18 P.M. on July 20, the *Eagle* landed on the moon in the Sea of Tranquility. The two astronauts spent 21 hours and 37 minutes on the moon. They started back to earth at 1:55 P.M. on July 21.

ORGANIZATION

Outlining

The following incomplete outline of the model composition is in chronological order. Can you complete it?

Outline of Model Composition 5

Main idea sentence. The first manned flight to the moon began when Apollo 11 blasted off from Cape Kennedy, Florida, at 9:32 A.M., on July 16, 1969, with Armstrong, Aldrin, and Collins as the astronauts.

1. On July 20, Armstrong and Aldrin moved from the command module into the lunar module.
2. The lunar module descended toward the moon.
3. _____
   _____
4. _____
   _____
5. The astronauts started back to earth at 1:55 P.M. on July 21.

EXERCISE 5-A Being Precise

The following report contains some imprecise information. Read it and underline the information which could be more exact. Then rewrite the report below, making the imprecise date more exact.

Sometime last week, Stephen Wosko hijacked a Pacific Southwest 727 in a city in California. He held some crew members hostage for several hours until he finally surrendered to the FBI. Before he surrendered, he read a statement saying that he had hijacked the plane in order to protest the govenment's recent foreign policy statements.

Rewritten Paragraph:

_____

_____

_____

_____

_____

_____

_____

_____

_____

_____

EXERCISE 5-B Irrelevant Sentences

Read the following reports. Find the sentence in each paragraph which does not support the main idea sentence. Cross it out.

1. On the night of April 14, 1912, during its first trip from England to New York City, the *Titanic* struck an iceberg in the North Atlantic Ocean and sank. The North Atlantic is now patrolled by the Coast Guard. The tragedy occurred about 1,600 miles (2,560 kilometers) northeast of New York City. The 66,000

OBJECTIVE REPORTING   65

ton (60,060 metric tons) ship was carrying 1,316 passengers and a crew of 891. There were not enough lifeboats for everybody, and hundreds of people jumped into the icy waters. No one knows exactly how many people died.

2. At 7:30 A.M. on March 28, 1979, there was a report of a severe accident in the No. 2 reactor at the Three Mile Island Nuclear Power Plant near Middletown, Pennsylvania. Radioactive gases were escaping through the plant's venting system, and there was a large hydrogen bubble in the top of the reactor. Nuclear experts announced the possibility of an explosion. On March 30, Pennsylvania's governor, Richard Thornburgh, closed twenty-three schools in the area and ordered pregnant women and pre-school children to leave the area. Radiation produced by X-rays is also dangerous to unborn babies. The crisis lasted thirteen days.

3. On May 18, 1980, Mount St. Helens erupted violently. The volcano sent hot mud, ash, and gases down its sides. Thick ash clouds rose 12 miles (19.2 kilometers) above the earth and turned day into night over a large area of the state of Washington. The explosion leveled 25,000 acres (10,000 hectares) of timber, destroyed dozens of homes, and washed out numerous bridges and roads. The damage was estimated at almost one billion dollars. At least 32 people died in the disaster. In 1979, the eruption of Mt. Simila in the Batur district of central Java killed 175 people.

GRAMMAR AND PUNCTUATION

Additional Uses of the Comma

In addition to the uses of the comma which you have already learned, commas are used with dates, with names of places, and with numerals to separate thousands.

DATES

Use a comma to separate a day from a month:
    Wednesday, July 16   Sunday, May 4

Use a comma to separate a date from a year:
    June 13, 1980   May 1, 1952

Use a comma after a year that follows a date:
    July 16, 1969, was the date of the Apollo 11 lift-off.
    My sister got married on July 8, 1960, in Baltimore.

Don't use a comma between a month and a year:
    November 1975   February 1950

PLACE NAMES

Use a comma to separate a city from a state or a city from a country:
    Houston, Texas   Paris, France

Use a comma after a state that follows a city:
    Cleveland, Ohio, is my hometown.

NUMERALS

Use a comma with numerals to separate thousands:
    10,000   77,850   244,930

EXERCISE 5-C

Put a comma where necessary in the following sentences. Some sentences include uses of the comma which you learned in previous sections.

1. On April 30 1978 Naomi Uemura became the first man to reach the North Pole alone by dog sled.
2. John Kennedy thirty-fifth president of the United States was born on May 29 1917 in Brookline Massachusetts.
3. On April 18 1979 the United States Senate voted to turn over the Panama Canal to Panama by a vote of 68 to 32.
4. The United States Japan and forty-seven other nations signed the Japanese Peace Treaty in San Francisco California on September 8 1951.
5. An overcrowded bus fell into Lake Victoria on July 14 1979.
6. In Youngstown Ohio four hundred municipal employees walked off their jobs on Wednesday April 6.
7. Over 65000 people marched in Washington on May 6 1979 to protest the use of nuclear power.
8. On November 19 1978 911 followers of the People's Temple Cult died in the Guyana jungle after drinking poisoned Kool-Aid.
9. In 1906 San Francisco California experienced one of the worst earthquakes in American history.
10. After the elevator was invented in the 1860s city buildings began to be built higher than five stories.

OBJECTIVE REPORTING **67**

Indirect Speech

In the last section, you learned that when you indirectly report a statement made in the *present* tense, you must change it to the *past* tense. Similarly, when you report a statement made in the **present continuous tense**, you must change it to the **past continuous tense**. Remember that a present continuous verb is formed with *am/is/are* + verb + *ing* (I *am listening,* she *is studying,* they *are sleeping*). A past continuous verb is formed with *was/were* + verb + *ing* (I *was listening,* she *was studying,* they *were sleeping.*)

EXAMPLES

Direct Speech: Pedro said, "I *am studying* chemical engineering."
Indirect Speech: Pedro said (that) he *was studying* chemical engineering.

Direct Speech: Mira told me, "I *am doing* a report in my writing class."
Indirect Speech: Mira told me (that) she *was doing* a report in her writing class.

EXERCISE 5-D

Change the following statements to indirect speech, using all the information in parentheses. Notice that some of the statements are in the present continuous tense while others are in the simple present tense. Use *said, told* or *announced,* as appropriate, to introduce the reported statements.

1. "We're flying over the Atlantic Ocean."
   (an hour after takeoff, the stewardess ⟶ the passengers)

   An hour after take-off, the stewardess told the passengers that they were flying over the Atlantic Ocean.

2. "When I want to read a novel, I write one."
   (Benjamin Disraeli, one of Britian's most distinguished prime ministers)

   Benjamin Disraeli, one of Britain's most distinguished prime ministers, said that when he wanted to read a novel, he wrote one.

3. "I'm an introvert in an extrovert profession."
   (during his presidency, Richard Nixon ⟶ friends)

4. "When I am working on a book or a story, I write every morning as soon after first light as possible."
   (Ernest Hemingway)

5. "I belong to the gods."
   (Isadora Duncan, a famous dancer)

6. "I have nothing to declare except my genius."
   (in 1882, Oscar Wilde, English playwright ⟶ New York customs officials)

7. "I am embarking on a wide ocean . . ."
    (in 1775, shortly after his election, George Washington ⟶ an audience)

8. "I am the greatest."
    (at the height of his boxing career, Muhammad Ali)

9. "I want to bind up the nation's wounds."
    (after the Civil War, Abraham Lincoln ⟶ Americans)

10. "I am reading the press more and enjoying it less."
    (during his presidency, John Kennedy)

STUDENT OUTLINE 5
The First Nonstop Solo Transatlantic Flight

Charles Lindbergh was the first person to fly alone across the Atlantic Ocean. These pictures give you some information about his historic flight. Use them to guide you in writing an outline for a report on this event. Write a main idea sentence and at least one sentence for each picture. Use the first picture for your main idea sentence. Make your information detailed and precise.

Helpful vocabulary: takeoff (n), take off (v)
pilot
parachute
radio
fly over (countries)
in _____ hours
land at
greet
medal
national hero
symbol of aviation

Main idea sentence: _____

_____

_____

_____

_____

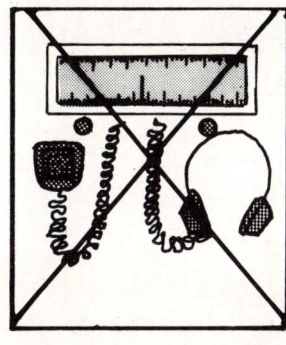

OBJECTIVE REPORTING **71**

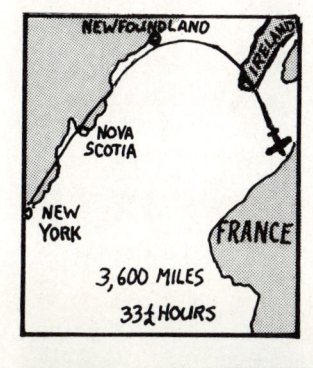

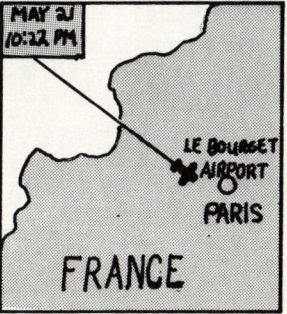

1.

2.

3.

4.

5.

6.

STUDENT COMPOSITION 5
The First Nonstop Solo Transatlantic Flight

Stepping Along

Step 1: Use your main idea sentence and outline to help you write a one-paragraph report. Be precise, and use correct punctuation.

Step 2: Exchange your composition with a partner. As you read your partner's report, think about these questions:
-Is everything in this report clear to you?
-Has your partner included all important details?
-Is the punctuation correct?
-Can you give your partner any suggestions for improvement?

Step 3: Talk with your partner about your compositions. Try to agree on improvements you can make.

Step 4: Rewrite your composition, making any changes you feel are necessary.

Further steps: As directed by your teacher.

MODEL COMPOSITION 6
Independence Day in Middleburg

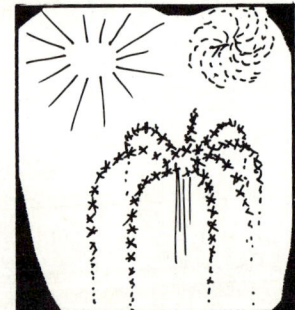

On July 4, Middleburg held its annual Independence Day celebration. A parade left City Hall at 10:45 A.M. The Calvin High School Band marched at the head of the parade. Firefighters from Station 29, Boy Scouts from Troop 240, and majorettes from Seabrook Junior High School were also among the participants. At 12:20 P.M., the parade reached Ambrose Park, where Mayor Rita Pasquarelli addressed the crowd. Mayor Pasquarelli said that Independence Day was a proud day for all Americans. After the speech, there were games and races in the park from 2 until 4 P.M. Jeffrey Boyd won the pie-eating contest. Wilma Petrov won the potato-sack race, and Joan and James Bonney finished first in the three-legged race. Mayor Pasquarelli awarded prizes to the winners. A softball game between Calvin High School and Woodrow High School followed. The team from Woodrow High School, the Tigers, won the game 7 to 3. At 6:30 P.M., the picnic started. Afterwards, from 7:30 to 9:30, the band played dance music. The celebration ended with a fireworks display.

ORGANIZATION

Outlining

Examine carefully the partial outline of the model composition. Can you complete it?

Outline of Model Composition 6

Main idea sentence. On July 4, Middleburg held its annual Independence Day celebration.

1. A parade left City Hall at 10:45 A.M.
   a. The Calvin High School Band marched at the head.
   b. Firefighters from Station 29, Boy Scouts from Troop 240, and majorettes from Seabrook Junior High School participated.
2. The parade reached Ambrose Park at 12:20 P.M.
3. Mayor Pasquarelli addressed the crowd.
   —She said that Independence Day was a proud day for all Americans.
4. There were games and races in the park from 2 until 4 P.M.
   a. Jeffrey Boyd won the pie-eating contest.
   b. Wilma Petrov won the potato-sack race.
   c. Joan and James Bonney finished first in the three-legged race.
5. Mayor Pasquarelli awarded prizes.
6. *A softball game between Calvin & Woodward followed*
   —The Tigers won.
7. The picnic started at 6:30.

8. _____

_____

9. _____

_____

For what audience was this report probably written? How do you know?

Major Points and Additional Details

As you have learned, a main idea sentence must be followed by major points. As your compositions become longer and more developed, the major points will be followed by additional details. These details give additional information about the major points. Additional details will make your composition more interesting and more complete.

In a report, the major points are the events. In a longer report, additional details about the events can be included. Here is an example from the model composition of a major point followed by additional details.

EXAMPLE

Major point: A parade left the City Hall at 10:05 A.M.
Additional details: a. The Calvin High School Band marched at the head of the parade.
                     b. Firefighters from Station 29, Boy Scouts from Troop 240, and majorettes from Seabrook Junior High School were among the participants.

The major point mentions an event (the parade). Statements *a* and *b* give details about it—they tell specific things about the parade.

Now read the model composition again. Find the statements which give additional details about events.

EXERCISE 6-A

In the following reports, underline each major point twice. Underline each statement which gives additional detail once. The first sentence in each report is the main idea sentence.

1. The Royal Oak Art Festival took place last week. The festival began at 9:30 A.M. on August 9 with a speech by the director of the Artists' Guild,

<u>Meredith Ainsley.</u> She welcomed everyone to the ninth annual festival. There was entertainment on the stage for the next hour. First, the Polish Folk Organization presented some traditional dances. After that, a group of children from Oakmont Elementary School gave a short play. At 10:30, local artists opened their booths and began a program of craft demonstrations. Ronald Taylor, a local glassblower, demonstrated the art of glass-blowing. Viola Eggars, a weaver, demonstrated the use of the loom. At noon, the food booths opened, and many types of ethnic food were sold. The Greek booth sold lamb shish-ka-bob, spinach pie, and baklava. The Japanese booth sold sushi and sukiyaki, and the Polish booth sold stuffed cabbage. The festival closed at 8:00 P.M.

2.   On August 30, 1979, Hurricane David began a week of destruction in the Caribbean and in parts of the U.S. The savage storm ripped across the islands of Dominica and Puerto Rico on August 30. Scores of people were left dead, injured, or homeless. On August 31, the hurricane headed north and struck the Dominican Republic. More than 1,000 people were killed, and thousands were injured. The 100 mile-per-hour winds and huge tides destroyed crops, power lines, and water supplies. In addition, an estimated 100,000 people lost their homes. On September 3, Hurricane David hit Florida near Palm Beach. Power lines were knocked out, and buildings and cars suffered heavy damage. The following day, the storm headed inland, across the islands off the coast of Georgia. It reached the Northeast on September 7. The storm ripped power lines throughout the area and cut off electricity for more than 2.5 million people in New York. Eight deaths were reported.

EXERCISE 6-B Main Idea Sentences

Read through each short report; then write an appropriate main idea sentence.

1. _____

_____

OBJECTIVE REPORTING 79

_____

_____

_____

The three prisoners captured the sheriff when he brought in a new prisoner. Jail officials then cut off the water supply, and the prisoners in turn threatened to kill the sheriff. On October 16, two days after the prisoners had seized the sheriff, they surrendered. Sheriff Olivetti was unharmed. Officials at the Kent Country Jail say the prisoners must stand trial.

2. _____

_____

_____

The mayor gave a campaign speech at the Lone Pine Motel early last evening. After the speech, he left the motel. Mayor Crosby returned about 2:00 A.M. Witnesses say he then banged loudly on the door of Harold Ruiz' room. When Ruiz opened the door, the mayor pulled out a gun and shot him. He immediately surrendered to authorities, claiming Ruiz had been blackmailing him.

3. _____

_____

_____

_____

_____

Beame, a maintenance worker for the Skyway Building, was washing the second-floor windows early Tuesday morning when he lost his balance and tumbled to the ground. Witnesses called an ambulance, and Beame was rushed to Montgomery County Hospital. Emergency room personnel announced that both his legs were paralyzed. Doctors now say that he will regain the use of his legs.

GRAMMAR AND PUNCTUATION

Capitalization

Capitalization is often required in English. Here are some examples of words or phrases which are capitalized.

First words of sentences:
Several students jogged through the park.

Names of people:
Marie Curie, Karl Marx

Specific places and locations:
Central Park, New York, United States

Streets:
Fifth Avenue, Scott Street

Schools:
Boston University, Lake Taylor High School

Nationalities:
American, Venezuelan

Languages:
Arabic, Japanese

Song titles:
"The Star-Spangled Banner," "Yesterday"

Book titles:
For Whom the Bell Tolls, Animal Farm

Holidays:
Thanksgiving, Valentine's Day

Organizations:
United Nations, Pittsburgh Steelers

Days of the week and months:
Tuesday, Saturday, June, August

Names and titles of people:
President Kennedy, Professor Steinmann, Ms. Whitehurst

EXERCISE 6-C

Circle the letters that need to be capitalized in the following paragraphs.

1. arlington national cemetery in arlington, virginia, contains the remains of many important americans. president john fitzgerald kennedy was buried there on november 25, 1963. the remains of his brother, senator robert f. kennedy, were laid to rest near him on june 8, 1968. soldiers from every war are also buried in arlington cemetery. on november 11, 1921, an unknown soldier from the first world war was interred there, and on memorial day, may 30, 1958, two unidentified soldiers from later wars were buried near him.

2. on may 28, lisa johns graduated from eastern michigan university in ypsilanti, michigan. she is the daughter of mr. and mrs. harold johns of frankstown road in pittsburgh. ms. johns majored in music and wrote an original song, ''late night blues,'' for her senior project. she plans to spend the summer traveling in france.

3. the famous pop group known as the beatles first played together in liverpool, england, in 1961. they made thirteen albums and three movies and greatly influenced a generation of young people. on august 26, 1966, the beatles gave their last concert at candlestick park in san francisco. the group recorded its last album, *let it be,* in 1970.

EXERCISE 6-D Punctuation Review

Punctuate the following sentences correctly. Be prepared to explain why you used the punctuation as you did.

1. Rudolph Diesel a German engineer invented the diesel engine in 1895.

2. Before you wax your car make sure it is completely dry.

3. The four most common names in the United States are Smith Johnson Williams and Brown.

4. At the corner of Wood and Fifth a truck hit a Greyhound bus.

5. On August 21 1959 Hawaii was admitted to the U.S. as its fiftieth state.

6. Check your arrival and departure dates carefully before you make your reservations.

7. Remove the cake from the pan when it is done and place it on a rack to cool.

8. America's first earth-orbiting space station Skylab crashed down in the Indian Ocean and on parts of Australia on July 11 1979.

9. After you loosen the dirt in your garden with a hoe use a rake to remove the rocks and weeds.

10. Caviar a delicacy of fish eggs is produced only in Russia Iran and Rumania.

11. In 1895 21-year-old Guglielmo Marconi made the world's first radio in Bologna Italy.

12. Be sure to tip the waiter before you leave the restaurant.

STUDENT OUTLINE AND COMPOSITION 6

Develop your own topic, or choose one of the topics below for a final report. You will be writing to inform your classmates about an event. Imagine that you are writing this report for your school newspaper. Think like a reporter.

1. Tell what occurred at a specific holiday (or wedding) celebration in your country.
2. Report on a significant historical event (political, social, or scientific) which took place in your country.
3. Tell what happened at an accident (automobile, fire, etc.) which you recently witnessed.
4. *CHALLENGER:* Think of a recent news event which interests you. It may be of local, national, or international importance (perhaps a sports event, a space journey, a crime, an accident, a political meeting, a birth, a death, etc.) Read about it in newspapers and newsmagazines and/or listen to TV or radio news. Take notes about the event, and *in your own words,* explain what happened.

Stepping Along

Step 1: After choosing your topic, take time to think and write a chronological outline of your major points.

Step 2: Form groups of about 3 students. Take turns reading your outlines to each other. Stop each other and ask questions when you think a point is missing or when something is not clear. Tell each other where you are interested in knowing additional details.

Step 3: Use your outline and your partners' suggestions to write your report. Consider your partners as your *audience.*

Step 4: When you finish writing, get into the same group of 3 students. Read both of your partners' reports. As you read each report, think about these questions:
-Would you like to know more details about any part of the report?
-Is there any part of the report which is not completely clear to you?
-Could this report be used in your school newspaper as it is written?
-Can you give your partner suggestions for improvement?

Step 5: Talk with your partners about these questions. Try to agree on improvements which you can make.

Step 6: Rewrite your composition, making any changes you feel are necessary.

Further steps: As directed by your teacher.

UNIT THREE
Analyzing by Cause and Effect

INTRODUCTION

In this unit, you will learn to look at an event or situation **(effect)** and examine the reasons or **causes** behind it. You analyze the cause of a situation when you wonder why your new shirt shrank or why you received a bad grade in a course. Sometimes there is only one obvious cause for an effect. For example, your 100-percent cotton shirt shrank because you washed it in hot water. Frequently, however, there is more than one probable cause of a situation, and it is important to examine all of them. Perhaps you received a bad grade in a course because you were absent too many times, got a D on your term paper, and failed your final exam. When you look at *multiple* causes, there is often one cause that is the most important. If your final exam counted for 75 percent of your final grade, that was the main reason you got a bad grade in your course.

When you analyze the cause of an effect, remember the following things.

1. *Examine all the causes.* If an event or situation has more than one cause, discuss all of them. If the economy of a country is failing, for example, there are probably several reasons.
2. *Support all the causes.* Give good examples to support each cause. For example, if one reason for a government's unpopularity is that it has passed certain laws, you need to give at least one example of these laws.
3. *Save your most important cause for last.* This makes your paper more interesting and gives it a strong conclusion. Also, if you put the most important cause first, your reader may feel it is not necessary to continue reading.
4. *Don't make judgments.* Be objective. A cause-effect composition doesn't recommend how to change the situation or give opinions about why the situation is good or bad. It simply examines the reasons for it.

People in all fields make use of this kind of organization when they write. A political science student, for example, might be asked to explain why a government fell. An ecologist might need to analyze why a particular lake or stream is polluted. Or a civil engineer might have to examine the reasons for the collapse of a certain bridge. In all of these cases, the purpose for writing is the same: to explain *why*.

MODEL COMPOSITION 7
Why Blake College Is Popular

Many students apply for admission to Blake College, and there are several reasons for its popularity. First of all, the campus is beautiful. It has many trees, a lot of grass, and handsome, well-kept buildings. In addition, the college has excellent facilities, such as a new gymnasium, a computer room, and a large library. On the weekends, there are always numerous extracurricular activities to choose from, such as films, lectures, dances, and concerts. The tuition, moreover, is only $500.00 per semester. But the major reason for the popularity of Blake College is its outstanding faculty. Classes are interesting and informative, and the professors are always willing to help after class.

ORGANIZATION

Outlining

The following outline shows the organization of the model composition. Examine it closely. Notice that there are five major points. There are also additional details which give more information about each of these points. (You will learn more about adding details in this section.) The main idea sentence gives the *effect;* the major points list the *causes.*

Outline of Model Composition 7

Main idea sentence. Many students apply for admission to Blake College, and there are several reasons for its popularity.

1. The campus is beautiful.
    a. Many trees
    b. A lot of grass
    c. Handsome, well-kept buildings
2. There are good facilities.
    a. A new gymnasium
    b. A computer room
    c. A large library
3. There are numerous extracurricular activities on the weekends.
    a. Films
    b. Lectures
    c. Dances
    d. Concerts
4. The tuition is inexpensive—$500.00 per semester.
5. The faculty is outstanding.
    a. Interesting and informative classes
    b. Helpful professors

When you write to explain the causes of a situation, it is effective to save the most important cause for the end of the composition. The writer of the model composition feels that the outstanding faculty (point 5 in the outline) is the main reason for the popularity of Blake College and ends the composition strongly with this point.

Understanding the Cause-Effect Relationship

In this unit, you will learn to explain the cause or causes of an effect. The following examples show the cause-effect relationship. Notice that an effect can have more than one cause.

EXAMPLES

1a. He feels tired today.   (effect)
    Why?
1b. He did not sleep well last night.   (cause)

2a. My car will not start.   (effect)
    Why?
2b. I left the car lights on all night.   (cause)

3a. The police are on strike.   (effect)
    Why?
3b. They want a salary increase.   (cause)
3c. They want additional health benefits.   (cause)
3d. They want more vacation time.   (cause)

EXERCISE 7-A

Decide which statement is the *cause* and which is the *effect*.

1. *cause*   The roads were icy.
   effect   There were many accidents.

2. _____   Jim stopped smoking cigarettes.
   _____   The price of cigarettes went up.

3. _____   The experiment succeeded.
   _____   The experiment was conducted carefully.

4. _____   Lucy is happy.
   _____   Lucy won the lottery.

5. _____ There was a severe storm last night.
   _____ Many buildings were damaged.
6. _____ The plants were not watered for a month.
   _____ The plants died.

EXERCISE 7-B

For each of the following situations, read the accompanying statements carefully. Circle the statement or statements which are possible causes of the situation.

1. The Eberlee Pharmacy is a very successful business operation.
    a. The clerks are friendly and helpful.
    b. The merchandise is reasonably priced.
    c. The owners work hard.

2. The majority of students failed the history test which Professor Dunn gave yesterday.
    a. The test was difficult.
    b. The students didn't study.
    c. Many students are enrolled in Professor Dunn's class.

3. The Lima City Council decided to cancel its August meeting.
    a. The city council has thirty active members.
    b. Many of the council members take a vacation in August.
    c. Each monthly meeting lasts approximately three hours.

4. The new wing of the San Diego Library, scheduled to be completed in 1978, was not completed until 1980.
    a. The construction workers were on strike for nearly a year.
    b. The library was noisy during the period of construction.
    c. The bricks needed for construction were delivered eight months late.

5. Flight #54 from Los Angeles to Chicago was postponed for two hours.
    a. Los Angeles has a very large airport.

b. The pilot of the plane became ill.

c. The plane seats 200 people.

Major Points and Additional Details

Remember that when you write, you must support your main idea sentence with *major points*. When you analyze the cause of a situation, your main idea sentence will tell the situation or *effect,* and your major points will tell the *causes.* In the outline of the model composition, sentences 1,2,3,4, and 5 are the major points. These major points are repeated below.

EXAMPLE

Main idea sentence. Many students apply for admission to Blake College, and there are several reasons for its popularity.

1. The campus is beautiful.
2. There are good facilities.
3. There are numerous extracurricular activities on the weekends.
4. The tuition is inexpensive—$500.00 per semester.
5. The faculty is outstanding.

However, if the composition included only the above major points, it would sound incomplete. A good cause-effect composition needs additional details. Look back at the outline of the model composition. Notice how additional details are added to each major point. Sometimes additional details follow in the next sentence. Sometimes they are included in the same sentence with the major point.

EXERCISE 7-C

Read the following cause-effect paragraphs. Underline twice each major point. Underline once the sentences or parts of sentences which give additional details. The first sentence of each paragraph is the main idea sentence.

1.   There are four major reasons why I like New York City. First of all, I think it is a beautiful city. It is filled with sleek glass skyscrapers, charming, old stone buildings, and attractive parks and squares. Second, I enjoy the cultural life which New York offers. Exciting concerts, Broadway plays, and new films are always available, as are museum exhibitions from all over the world. In addition, I appreciate the light entertainment the city offers. Nowhere else in the United States

can one find so many delightful restaurants, nightclubs, cabarets, and discotheques. Finally, I like the diversity of people in New York City. The city has the largest tourist population in the world. It also has colorful ethnic neighborhoods such as Little Italy, Harlem, Spanish Harlem, and Chinatown.

2.   There are a number of known causes of cancer. Excessive exposure to radiation is one of the most common causes of skin cancer. The sun's rays contain radiation. So do X-rays. Exposure to toxic substances is another of the many causes of this disease. Asbestos, for example, is associated with lung cancer, and vinyl chloride has been linked to liver cancer. Smoking is probably the most well-known cause. Cigarettes, cigars, and pipes are responsible for lip, throat, and lung cancer.

EXERCISE 7-D

Below, outlines of the preceding paragraphs have been started. Complete the outlines, showing both the major points and the additional details.

1. **Main idea sentence.** There are four major reasons why I like New York City.

   1. *I think it is a beautiful city.*
      a. *Sleek glass skyscrapers*
      b. *Charming, old stone buildings*
      c. *Attractive parks and squares*

CAUSE AND EFFECT 93

2. **Main idea sentence.** There are a number of known causes of cancer.

1. Excessive exposure to radiation is one of the most common causes.
a. Sun's rays

Main Idea Sentence

A main idea sentence for a cause-effect composition usually tells the reader 1) what the event or situation is and 2) that there are causes or reasons for the situation. The number of causes is also mentioned (such as *several reasons, two major causes, three important reasons*).

EXAMPLES

    ┌────── effect ──────┐┌────── causes ──────┐
Accidents involving aircraft occur for a variety of reasons.

    ┌────── causes ──────┐┌────── effect ──────┐
There are three causes for her lack of success in the course.

EXERCISE 7-E

Read the following cause-effect paragraphs carefully. Then circle the best main idea sentence for each.

1. First, the classroom is uncomfortable. It is very warm, and there are no windows for ventilation. In addition, the class meets at 8:00 A.M. This hour is too early for most college students. Most important of all, students seldom attend this class because of the teacher. He is an unpleasant, humorless man, and his lectures are boring.

   a. The poor attendance in Professor O'Toole's class has several causes.
   b. There are several reasons the classroom is uncomfortable.
   c. Students do not attend Professor O'Toole's class.

2. First, because of automation, many Americans get little or no exercise. The automobile, especially, is to blame. Driving is faster and easier than walking but does not keep the body trim. In addition, the diet of many Americans is responsible for obesity. Such fattening foods as hamburgers, French fries, cakes, and cookies are common foods in the American diet.

   a. Americans should get more exercise and eat better food.
   b. A large percentage of Americans are overweight for two major reasons.
   c. Americans should drive less for two major reasons.

3. First of all, Americans are moving to escape the cold and the snow of the North. The Southwest offers warmth and sun almost year-round, and this gentle climate allows people to be much more active outdoors. Furthermore, because of the warm climate, the cost of heating a home in the Southwest is much less than in the North, and many Americans move in order to save heating costs. And finally, many Americans are tired of the crowds and the stress in the northern cities. They relocate in the Southwest hoping to find freedom and peace in its wide-open spaces.

   a. Americans are moving for several reasons.
   b. Americans do not like snow for several reasons.
   c. There are several reasons why many Americans are moving from northern states to southwestern states such as Texas and Arizona.

Transitions Showing Addition

When you are listing causes or other ideas in a composition, you should use transitions which show addition in order to introduce your major points. The following transitions are appropriate for a composition which lists several causes for an event. Notice the punctuation used with each.

>First (of all,) . . .
>Another reason is . . .
>In addition, . . .
>Also, . . .
>Moreover, . . .
>The major (most important) reason is/Finally, . . .

In addition and *moreover* do not always appear at the beginning of the sentence. Note the following examples.

EXAMPLES

In addition, the college has excellent facilities.
The college, *in addition*, has excellent facilities.

Moreover, the tuition is expensive.
The tuition, *moreover*, is expensive.

EXERCISE 7-F

Underline the transitions used in Model Composition 7.

EXERCISE 7-G

The following cause-effect paragraph is poorly written because it lacks transitions. It would be much easier to understand if transitions were used between its major points. Decide where each major supporting statement begins, and insert appropriate transitions. Do not use the above transitions between a major point and a sentence which gives additional detail about the major point. Rewrite the paragraph in the space provided below.

There are three reasons Mr. Tucker was fired from his job. He was often absent from work. He missed thirty working days last year. His personality was a problem. He was nasty to other employees and to the customers. His performance on the job was poor. He did not follow the boss' instructions, and he rarely completed assignments.

Rewritten Paragraph:

_____

_____

_____

_____

_____

_____

_____

EXERCISE 7-H

Now do the same with this paragraph.

Superfair is the most popular supermarket in town for several reasons. The store has a large selection of items. You can find any food you want, even the rarest spice or the most exotic fruit. The prices are very reasonable. A gallon of milk costs no more here than in any other supermarket. Meat costs even less! There are no long waiting lines at the check-out counter. Check-out time is usually no more than five minutes.

Rewritten Paragraph:

_____

_____

_____

STUDENT OUTLINE 7
Why Croft College Is Unpopular

Imagine that an overseas friend of yours is considering applying to Croft College, a college which you know is very unpopular. You must try to explain to your friend why it is a poor choice. These pictures show you five major reasons for the college's unpopularity. Write an outline and main idea sentence. Add at least one additional detail to each of your five major points. Use the outline of Model Composition 7 as a guide.

    Helpful vocabulary: trash/garbage
                                    cracked (concrete)
                                    run-down (buildings)
                                    outdated (books)
                                    expensive (tuition)
                                    boring (classes)
                                    not helpful (teachers)

Main idea sentence: _____

_____

_____

_____

1.

CAUSE AND EFFECT 99

2.

3.

4.

5.

STUDENT COMPOSITION 7
Why Croft College Is Unpopular

Stepping Along

Step 1: Use your main idea sentence and your outline to help you write a one-paragraph composition. Use appropriate transitions to introduce each major point.

Step 2: Exchange your composition with a partner. With a pencil, lightly underline *twice* each major point in your partner's composition. Underline *once* each additional detail.
-Did your partner use details to support the major points?
-Did your partner use transitions before major points?
-Can you give your partner any suggestions for improvement?

Step 3: Talk with your partner about your compositions. Try to agree on improvements which you can make.

Step 4: Rewrite your composition, making any changes you feel are necessary.

Further steps: As directed by your teacher.

MODEL COMPOSITION 8
Why Sandra Miller Is Not Healthy

There are several factors which might explain my friend Sandra Miller's poor health. First of all, Sandra seldom eats properly. Her favorite foods are pizza, potato chips, cookies, and candy bars. Second, she gets very little exercise. She drives her car everywhere and prefers watching sports to participating in them. She also seldom gets enough rest. She works late into the night and gets up early. She has, moreover, several bad habits such as excessive smoking and coffee-drinking which make her nervous. But the most important cause of Sandra's ill health is probably her job. She feels a great deal of stress and cannot enjoy her work because she has too much to do. She never has enough time to answer all her mail, return all her phone calls, and write all her reports.

ORGANIZATION

Outlining

Examine carefully the partial outline of the model composition. How many major points are there? Can you complete the outline?

Outline of Model Composition 8

Main idea sentence. There are several factors which might explain my friend Sandra Miller's poor health.

1. Sandra seldom eats properly.
   a. Eats pizza
   b. Eats potato chips
   c. *Eats cookies*
   d. *Eats candy bars*
2. She gets very little exercise.
   a. Drives her car everywhere
   b. Doesn't participate in sports.
3. *She seldom gets enough rest*
   a. Works late
   b. Gets up early
4. She has several bad habits.
   a. *Smokes too much*
   b. *Drinks coffee*
5. Her job is stressful.
   a. Too much mail
   b. *Too many phone calls*
   c. Too many reports

104 BASIC COMPOSITION FOR ESL

EXERCISE 8-A Major Points and Additional Details

Below is a partial outline for a cause-effect composition. Notice that there are five major points which support the main idea sentence. Complete the outline by adding additional details to each of these major points.

Main idea sentence. There are several reasons for the popularity of Port Haven, the well-known seaside resort.

1. The resort is in a beautiful location.

   a. *On a hill next to the ocean*

   b.

2. There are many types of sporting activities available.

   a. *Golf*

   b.

   c.

   d.

3. The area offers several interesting historical sites.

   a.

   b.

4. In the evening, there are many different types of entertainment to choose from.

   a.

   b.

c.

5. Prices at the resort are reasonable.

   a.

   b.

The Cause-Effect Relationship

Many events or situations have more than one cause. Some causes are very important; others are less important. A thorough cause-effect composition, however, considers every cause.

EXERCISE 8-B

Practice thinking of multiple causes by writing three possible causes for the following effects.

1. Jack Nolte failed his physics exam.

   He often missed lectures during the semester.
   He forgot to do a portion of the exam.
   He had a headache during the exam.

2. Jane Feldman stopped smoking.

3. There are, on the average, over 700,000 fires per year in American homes and apartments.

4. Each year many foreign students come to American colleges and universities to study.

5. Some people would rather travel by bus than by plane.

6. Automobile accidents occur frequently on American highways.

EXERCISE 8-C Irrelevant Sentences

Read the following cause-effect paragraphs. Find a sentence in each paragraph which does not support the main idea sentence. Cross it out.

1. The Lilac Inn Restaurant is losing business for three major reasons. First, customers are staying away because of the insanitary conditions in the restaurant; the tables are often messy and the floors dirty. In addition, the service is poor. The waiters and waitresses are generally slow and unfriendly. The waiters and waitresses wear uniforms. Most important of all, customers are not pleased with the food at the Lilac Inn. The meals are of poor quality and overpriced.

2. There are several reasons why Henry Ford achieved such success with his automobile. The first reason is that Ford concentrated on making a single model (the Model-T Ford) and was thus able to perfect his product. Moreover, by introducing the assembly-line method to automobile production, he was able to improve production efficiency. Henry Ford also ran for the Senate but lost. Finally, he was successful because of the low price of his cars; in 1921, the cost per car was only $280.

3. For several reasons, jogging has become a very popular sport in the United States. First of all, in contrast to most other sports, jogging requires no real training. Joggers must only be able to put one foot in front of the other. Occasionally joggers have heart attacks. Americans also like jogging because it is not expensive. The only item they must buy is a pair of good running shoes. Finally, people like the sport because it is easy to observe the progress they are making.

GRAMMAR AND PUNCTUATION

Showing Cause-Effect with *Because*

At the sentence level, cause-effect is often expressed by two clauses connected with *because*. *Because* introduces the clause that gives the cause for a situation. This clause can be placed at the beginning or at the end of the sentence. Notice the punctuation in the examples.

EXAMPLES

Sandra cannot enjoy her job *because* she has too much work.

Because she has too much work, Sandra cannot enjoy her job.

EXERCISE 8-D

Decide first which sentence is the cause and which the effect. Then combine the sentences with *because*, changing nouns to pronouns where necessary. Write each sentence two ways.

1. DDT was discovered to be dangerous to animals and humans.
   DDT is now banned in the United States.

   DDT is now banned in the United States because it was discovered to be dangerous to animals and humans.

   Because DDT was discovered to be dangerous to animals and humans, it is now banned in the United States.

2. The workers went on strike.
   The workers were unhappy with their wages.

3. The car will not start.
   The battery is dead.

4. Michigan borders on four of the five Great Lakes.
   Michigan was nicknamed "The Great Lake State."

5. The man robbed a bank.
   The man was sent to prison.

EXERCISE 8-E

Complete the following sentences.

1. Because Jack needed money, *he got a part-time job washing cars*.

2. The student passed the test because _____

_____

3. Because _____

_____, the car slid.

4. We ate a big dinner because _____

_____

5. Because the television set is not plugged in, _____
_____ .

6. _____
_____ because she felt ill.

Punctuation with Adverbial Clause: Summary

The *because* clause is a dependent adverbial clause which tells *why*. In Unit One, you studied dependent adverbial clauses which tell *when:* clauses beginning with *before, after,* and *when.* These clauses can be placed at the beginning or the end of the sentence. When the clauses occur at the beginning of the sentence, a comma follows them.

EXAMPLES

When the omelet becomes firm, lay thin slices of cheese on it.

Lay thin slices of cheese on the omlet *when it becomes firm.*

Because she drinks a lot of coffee, she feels nervous.

She feels nervous *because she drinks a lot of coffee.*

EXERCISE 8-F

Punctuate these sentences correctly. Some need no additional punctuation.

1. After you cross the bridge turn right onto Lincoln Road.

2. In the 1960s many students in the United States participated in marches and demonstrations because they were opposed to the war in Vietnam.

3. Take the clothes out of the washer when the machine turns off.

4. Before you do the experiment check the equipment carefully.

5. Because he could no longer conceal his involvement in the Watergate scandal President Nixon resigned from office in 1974.

6. Deposit your money before you press the button.

7. When the American Civil War ended in 1864 the slaves were freed.

8. After the United States bought Alaska from Russia in 1867 gold and oil were discovered there.

STUDENT OUTLINE 8
Why Bob Adams Is Healthy

Suppose that Sandra Miller (from Model Composition 8) is a friend of yours and you want to persuade her to change her lifestyle. You have a mutual friend, Bob Adams, who is in good health. Explain to Sandra the reasons for Bob's good health. Write an outline with five major points and a main idea sentence. Add as much detail as possible to each major point.

Helpful vocabulary: well-balanced (meals)
vegetables
fruit
meat
exercise regularly
play baseball/tennis
alcohol
go to bed
get up
get along well with (co-workers)

Main idea sentence: _____

_____

_____

_____

1.

CAUSE AND EFFECT   **113**

2.

3.

114 BASIC COMPOSITION FOR ESL

4.

5.

STUDENT COMPOSITION 8
Why Bob Adams Is Healthy

Stepping Along

Step 1: Use your main idea sentence and your outline to help you write a one-paragraph composition. Use appropriate transitions to introduce each major point.

Step 2: Exchange your composition with a partner. With a pencil, lightly underline *twice* each major point in your partner's composition. Underline *once* each additional detail. Circle the transitions. As you read your partner's composition, think about these questions:
-Did your partner use details to support the major points?
-Did your partner use transitions appropriately?
-Can you give your partner any suggestions for improvement?

Step 3: Talk with your partner about your compositions. Try to agree on improvements which you can make.

Step 4: Rewrite your composition, making any changes you feel are necessary.

Further steps: As directed by your teacher.

MODEL COMPOSITION 9
The Causes of Famine

Famine, a serious problem today and in the past, has several different causes. One is drought. In 1866, a severe drought resulted in 1,500,000 deaths in India. Too much rainfall is another cause. In 1813, Poland suffered through a terrible famine because of weeks of continuous rain. Famine may also result from pests. Swarms of ants, for instance, attacked India's crops in 1791, and hordes of rats devoured most of the food there in 1812. Locusts, another common pest, cause starvation all over the world, especially in Africa, India, and China. In addition, famine can occur when a plant disease destroys the main food supply. Almost 750,000 people starved to death in Ireland in the 1840s because of a potato disease. The major reason for widespread starvation, however, is war. In wartime, people are fighting instead of working in the fields. The enemy may bomb food storehouses and blow up roads so that food cannot be transported. The situations in Biafra in the 1960s and Bangladesh in the 1970s are modern examples of an old problem.

ORGANIZATION

Outlining

Examine the outline for the model composition carefully. Notice that the major points are not written in complete sentences; this is a **topic outline**. A topic outline is a simplified outline of the major points that includes only key words. Read the composition again, and underline the sentences which give the major points.

Outline of Model Composition 9

Main idea sentence.   Famine, a serious problem today and in the past, has several different causes.

1. Drought—India, 1866
2. Too much rainfall—Poland, 1813
3. Pests
    a. India, 1719 (ants)
    b. India, 1812 (rats)
    c. Africa, India, China (locusts)
4. Plant disease—Ireland, 1840s (potato disease)
5. War
    a. Biafra, 1960s
    b. Bangladesh, 1970s

CAUSE AND EFFECT 119

EXERCISE 9-A Major Points and Additional Details

Read the following cause-effect paragraphs, and write at least one additional detail for each major point.

1. People seldom stay in the old Brandmire Hotel anymore for several reasons. First, the price of rooms is very high. *A double room costs over $75.00, and a single costs over $50.00.* Second, furnishings in the rooms are frequently broken or in poor repair. _____

    _____
    _____
    _____
    _____

    In addition, the hotel has no restaurant. _____

    _____
    _____
    _____

    Finally, the Brandmire Hotel is located in a dangerous section of town.

    _____
    _____
    _____
    _____

2. There are many reasons why English is a difficult language to learn. One reason is the use of prepositions. *For instance, "in," "on," and "at" are hard to learn.*

English speakers live "in" a city, "on" a street, and "at" an address!

In addition, there are many odd idiomatic expressions. _____

_____

_____

_____

_____

A third reason for the difficulty of English is its irregular spelling. Many words in the language sound the same but are written differently.

_____

_____

_____

_____

_____

Main Idea Sentences

Remember that a main idea sentence for a cause effect composition 1) tells the reader what the event or situation is and 2) mentions that there are causes or reasons for the situation.

EXERCISE 9-B

Read the following paragraphs carefully, and write a main idea sentence for each one.

1. _____

_____

_____

_____

First, more infants survive today than in the past, so people don't need to have as many children now. Second, more women have jobs. They have fewer babies because it is difficult to care for children and work too. Perhaps one of the most important reasons why Americans are having fewer children, however, is that the cost of raising a child is very high. Parents are afraid that they can't feed, clothe, and educate many children and are therefore limiting the size of their families.

2. _____

_____

_____

First, the population is increasing, and more gas and other fuels are being used. Second, the United States is not completely developing all its energy sources. For example, the use of coal has been limited because coal burning causes pollution. A third reason for the energy problem is America's dependence on oil from other countries. If these countries refuse to sell their oil, all Americans feel the effects. But probably the most important reason for the energy problem is that the United States has no acceptable alternate sources of energy. Both solar and nuclear power are possibilities, but solar power is not completely developed yet, and many people feel that nuclear power is dangerous.

3. _____

_____

_____

One reason is that the husband's income is often no longer enough to cover expenses because the cost of housing, food, and education has increased. Another important reason is that there are more single-parent families. Sadly, due to increased divorce rates, more women live alone with their children and must work to support them. However, the most important reason of all is probably that the traditional role of women is changing. American women are no longer satisfied to stay at home in their kitchens. Instead, they are going outside their homes to pursue careers in other fields.

GRAMMAR AND PUNCTUATION

Showing Cause-Effect with *Because of*

You have learned that cause-effect is often expressed by two clauses connected with *because*. Cause can also be expressed by *because of* + *noun or noun phrase*. (A **noun phrase** is a phrase which functions as a noun.) Examine this pattern carefully, and compare it with *because* + *clause*. Notice the punctuation.

EXAMPLES

Because + *clause:* Because there was a bad hailstorm, we couldn't get to work.

We couldn't get to work *because there was a bad hailstorm*.

Because of +
noun/noun phrase: Because of the bad hailstorm, we couldn't get to work.

We couldn't get to work *because of the bad hailstorm*.

EXERCISE 9-C

Rewrite each sentence, replacing *because* + *clause* with *because of* + *noun phrase*. Punctuate correctly.

1. *Because the divorce rate is high,* many children today are being raised by single parents.

   Because of the high divorce rate, many children today are being raised by single parents.

2. The school cancelled the baseball game *because there was a thunderstorm warning.*

   The school cancelled the baseball game because of a thunderstorm warning.

3. *Because its climate is bleak,* the Antarctic is uninhabited.

CAUSE AND EFFECT   **123**

4. More than 22,000 lives were lost in Guatemala in 1976 *because there was a major earthquake.*

5. They decided not to swim *because the current was rough.*

6. *Because the view is magnificent,* tourists enjoy visiting the Grand Canyon.

7. Al Capone was often called "Scarface" *because there was a conspicuous scar on his cheek.*

8. Many students apply to Yale University *because its reputation is excellent.*

EXERCISE 9-D

Fill in the blanks with an appropriate cause or effect. Use *because of* + *noun/noun phrase* when you fill in a cause.

1. A famine occurred in Ireland in the 1840s _____

_____

2. _____ because

of the bad weather.

3. Saul wasn't accepted at the university _____

_____

4. _____, Theresa always eats at Giordello's Restaurant.

5. _____ because of the low prices.

6. Paula wore a heavy sweater _____
_____

Showing Cause-Effect with *So* and *Therefore*

The cause-effect relationship can also be expressed with *so* or *therefore*. Both introduce the effect clause. Notice the punctuation used with these words.

EXAMPLE

Henrique received a large scholarship from his

government $\left\{\begin{array}{l}\text{, so}\\ \text{; therefore,}\\ \text{. Therefore,}\end{array}\right\}$ he can attend a good university.

So and *therefore* have the same meaning, but *therefore* is used for more formal writing.

EXERCISE 9-E

Decide which sentence expresses the cause and which expresses the effect. Then combine the sentences three ways, using *so* and both positions of *therefore*. Change nouns to pronouns where necessary.

1. Jim wants to be a top tennis player.
   Jim practices four hours a day.

Jim wants to be a top tennis player, so he practices four hours a day.
Jim wants to be a top tennis player; therefore, he practices four hours a day.

CAUSE AND EFFECT

Jim wants to be a top tennis player. Therefore, he practices four hours a day.

2. Mr. Peabody is allergic to cigarette smoke.
   Mr. Peabody has a "No Smoking" sign on his desk.

3. The Palmers moved from Wisconsin to Florida.
   The Palmers dislike harsh winters.

4. The Vermont ski resort lost money.
   The winter was mild in Vermont in 1980.

5. In the United States, houses are becoming more expensive every year.
   Many young families are renting apartments.

EXERCISE 9-F

As a review, finish the sentences by writing in your own ideas or feelings. Underline the appropriate word or phrase where you are given a choice of two.

1. _____ ; therefore,

   I am studying English.

2. I like/dislike the food in the United States because _____

   _____ .

3. _____ , so

   I'm in a good/bad mood today.

4. I study/do not study hard. Therefore, _____

   _____ .

5. _____ , so I

   got up early/late.

6. I feel tired/energetic today because _____

   _____ .

EXERCISE 9-G Punctuation Review

Punctuate these sentences correctly. Some need no additional punctuation.

1. Because Ms. Divens was an excellent teacher her classes were always full.

2. Americans can vote when they are eighteen years old.

3. The bald eagle the symbol of the United States is very rare so the United States government protects it.

4. Ms. Nicholes has an ulcer therefore she never eats spicy foods.

5. Because of the high crime rate in many cities a large number of Americans prefer to live in the suburbs.

6. More than 5000 people died in Pakistan in 1974 because of an earthquake.

7. On March 10 1876 Alexander Graham Bell first demonstrated the telephone.

8. The vaccine for rabies was discovered in 1885 by Louis Pasteur a French scientist.

9. The University of Michigan has over 46000 students.

STUDENT OUTLINE AND COMPOSITION 9

Develop your topic, or choose one of the following for your final cause-effect composition. Consider your fellow students as your audience.

1. Causes of air pollution
2. Why I like/dislike living in this city
3. Why I like/dislike attending this college
4. *CHALLENGER:* People who live in large cities have a shorter life expectancy than people who live in small towns. Why do you think this is so?

Stepping Along

Step 1: After choosing your topic, divide into pairs or small groups according to the topic you have chosen. Discuss the topic together. Try to generate as many ideas as possible.

Step 2: Together, write an outline of your ideas. Remember to add additional details to each of your major points.

Step 3: On your own, write a composition using your outline and main idea sentence. Remember to use transitions of addition (*first, also, in addition,* etc.) to introduce your major points.

Step 4: Exchange compositions with a new partner. As you read your partner's composition, think about these questions:
-What do you like best about the composition?
-Is everything in the composition clear to you?
-Has your partner supported each major point with at least one additional detail?
-Are transitions used appropriately?
-Can you give your partner any suggestions for improvement?

Step 5: Talk with your partner about your compositions. Try to agree on improvements which you can make.

Step 6: Rewrite your composition, making any changes which you feel are necessary.

Further steps: As directed by your teacher.

UNIT FOUR
Comparing and Contrasting

INTRODUCTION

Comparing and contrasting is something all of us frequently do. When you decide, for instance, whether to buy your friend's used motorcycle or a new one, whether to attend the university in New York or the one in California, or whether to rent the apartment near the university or the one downtown, you compare and contrast. **Comparing** means thinking or writing about the *similarities* between two things or people; **contrasting** means thinking or writing about their *differences*.

When you compare and contrast, you can organize your material in several different ways. In this unit, you will learn two simple arrangements.

Suppose you are interested in showing the differences between airplanes and helicopters. You will then write a contrast composition. When you are contrasting, however, it is effective to mention also the similarities between the two things you are contrasting. You should mention these similarities in your main idea sentence. If you wish, you may develop these similarities in a separate paragraph before going on to the differences.

One way to arrange your material (after writing your main idea sentence and discussing the similarities) is to write about airplanes in one paragraph and to write about helicopters in the next. If you mention a particular point in the airplane paragraph, you must mention the same point in the helicopter paragraph, and *in the same order*. Study the following outline which shows this kind of organization.

131

Introduction

(I. Similarities between airplanes and helicopters)

II. Airplanes
   A. Shape and design
   B. Speed
   C. Direction of takeoff and flight

III. Helicopters
   A. Shape and design
   B. Speed
   C. Direction of takeoff and flight

Conclusion

    A second way to organize this material is to discuss a particular point about airplanes and then immediately discuss the same point about helicopters. This is called a point-by-point arrangement. An outline of this arrangement follows.

Introduction

(I. Similarities between airplanes and helicopters)

II. Differences between airplanes and helicopters
   A. Shape and design
      1. Airplanes
      2. Helicopters
   B. Speed
      1. Airplanes
      2. Helicopters
   C. Direction of takeoff and flight
      1. Airplanes
      2. Helicopters

Conclusion

    When you become a more experienced writer, you may want to develop each point into a separate paragraph, but in this unit you will use a single paragraph for your point-by-point arrangements.
    When you want to emphasize the similarities between two things or two people, you may use these same arrangements.
    Both students and professionals frequently need to compare and contrast in order to explain something. A physics student, for instance, might explain fission and fusion by pointing out their differences and similarities. Similarly, an economist might find it useful to explain this year's table of economic growth by comparing and contrasting it with last year's table.

MODEL COMPOSITION 10
My Two Brothers

Most people assume that sisters and brothers have many things in common. This is not always true. Both my brothers, Nick and Joe, have the same parents and the same background, but they differ considerably in appearance and lifestyle.

Nick, the younger one, has long curly hair and a beard. He usually dresses casually in blue jeans and a T-shirt. He is a cook in a small restaurant. Because the restaurant is near his home, he rides his bicycle to work. In his free time, Nick goes to movies and plays football. He lives alone in the city in a studio apartment.

My brother Joe, on the other hand, looks more conservative than Nick. He has shorter, straighter hair. He has a mustache but no beard. His clothes are also more conservative than Nick's are. Because he is a businessman, he wears a suit and tie to work. He drives his car to his downtown office every day. In his spare time, he goes dancing and plays soccer. Joe lives in a large house in the suburbs with his wife, their children, and a cat.

My friends cannot believe that Nick and Joe are brothers because they seem so different.

ORGANIZATION

Outlining

A formal outline for a composition of more than one paragraph in length looks like the one below. The subject of each paragraph is written after a Roman numeral (I, II . . .), the major points after capital letters (A, B), and the additional details appear after numbers (1, 2 . . .). Although this is the form used in this text, many writers make a less formal plan before writing.

As mentioned in the introduction to this unit, there are different arrangements you can use when you compare and contrast. Model Composition 10 is organized into two major paragraphs: the first about Nick and the second about Joe.

I. Everything about Nick
   A.
   B.
   C.
   D.
   E.
   F.

II. Everything about Joe
   A.
   B.
   C.
   D.
   E.
   F.

In this kind of organization, keep your major points in the same order. If you write about appearance first in paragraph I, write about it first in paragraph II, and so on. Examine the following outline of the model composition carefully. Is it a sentence outline or a topic outline?

Outline of Model Composition 10

Introduction

I. Nick
   A. Appearance
      1. Long curly hair
      2. Beard
   B. Clothes
      1. Blue jeans
      2. T-shirt
   C. Job—cook
   D. Transportation—bicycle
   E. Free time
      1. Movies
      2. Football
   F. Housing—studio apartment in the city

II. Joe
   A. Appearance
      1. Shorter, straighter hair
      2. No beard
   B. Clothes
      1. Suit
      2. Tie
   C. Job—businessman
   D. Transportation—car
   E. Free time
      1. Dancing
      2. Soccer
   F. Housing—large house in the suburbs

Conclusion

Note: This composition has both an **introduction** and a **conclusion**. You will learn about introductions in this lesson and about conclusions in lesson 12.

Main Idea Sentences

A main idea sentence for a composition that compares and contrasts should tell the reader 1) what two things or people are being compared and contrasted, and 2) whether the composition will emphasize the similarities or the differences between them. Even if you wish to stress the differences in your main idea sentence, you should still mention the similarities, and vice versa. Often, words like *but* and *however* are used to connect the two parts of a main idea sentence for a comparison/contrast composition.

EXAMPLES

Study carefully these examples of main idea sentences for comparison/contrast compositions. Answer the following questions for each.

—What two things or people are being *compared* or *contrasted*?
—Will the composition emphasize the *similarities* or the *differences* between them?

Disneyland and Disneyworld are both products of the imagination of the same man, Walt Disney, *but* the two parks offer very different types of entertainment.

The political systems of the United States and my country seem different at first, *but* they actually have some striking similarities.

Many people think that humans have little in common with sea animals; *however,* scientists have shown that the dolphin resembles us in many ways.

EXERCISE 10-A

Read each short comparison/contrast composition carefully. Then choose the best main idea sentence for each.

1.   Airplanes have long, slender bodies with wings. They travel extremely fast, reaching speeds of over 1,875 miles (3,000 kilometers) per hour. Airplanes take off horizontally and can move in a forward direction only. They need a lot of space for takeoff and landing. Airplanes regularly carry several hundred passengers.
    Helicopters, on the other hand, have round bodies and propellers rather than wings. They move at much slower speeds than airplanes. They take off vertically and can move in any direction. Helicopters require a very small takeoff or landing space. Most helicopters carry only two-to-five passengers.

   a. Airplanes and helicopters are both important forms of air travel, but there are great differences between them.

b. Airplanes and helicopters are both important forms of air transportation; however, they do not travel at the same speeds.
c. Airplanes and helicopters have very different shapes but both carry passengers.

2. New York City is located on the East Coast of the United States. It is filled with skyscrapers which are concentrated in a relatively small area of 319 square miles (829 square kilometers). New York is known as the fashion center of the United States and also contains most of the publishing houses which select and print the nation's books.

Los Angeles is on the West Coast of the United States. This city is spread out over a much larger area of 464 square miles (1,206 square kilometers), and its buildings are much lower than the buildings in New York. Los Angeles is an important industrial center for the manufacture of aircraft and airplane parts. Los Angeles is also the capital of the movie industry.

a. The cities in the United States are different from those in other countries.
b. Los Angeles and New York are both large American cities, but they differ in major ways.
c. New York City and Los Angeles are both important cities in the United States; however, they are located on opposite coasts and have different-sized buildings.

3. Hitler, a dictator who believed in the superiority of the German people, built up Germany's military strength during the 1930s. His aim was to dominate Europe. He arrested people by the millions and sent them to concentration camps or executed them. Hitler involved Europe in a catastrophic war. When it became clear that Germany had lost, he is believed to have committed suicide.

Similarly, the dictator Mussolini craved power and wanted all the men of Italy to be soldiers. His aim was to build Italy into a great empire. Like Hitler, Mussolini kept control by means of murder, exile, and prison camps. He joined Hitler in the war and, when Italy was losing, was shot by his Italian opponents.

a. Hitler was a dictator of Germany, but Mussolini was a dictator of Italy.
b. Hitler and Mussolini ruled different countries; however, they both wanted power.
c. Hitler and Mussolini were heads of two different countries, but their dictatorships had much in common.

Introductions

Now that your compositions will be more than one paragraph in length, they should have an **introduction**. In short compositions, such as those you will be writing for this course, the introduction is only a few sentences in length and always includes the main idea sentence. A good introduction makes the reader want to continue reading.

An introduction introduces the subject generally. Then it specifies, in a main idea sentence, what particular points will be discussed in the composition. The introduction in the model composition introduces the subject of sisters and brothers in general and then goes on to talk about two particular brothers, Nick and Joe.

There are different ways to write an introduction. One way is to begin with a common belief and show that it is not always true. The main idea sentence then gives the particular points that will be discussed in the composition to prove that the common belief is not always true. This method is the one that has been used for the model composition.

> Most people assume that sisters and brothers have many things in common. This is not always true. Both my brothers, Nick and Joe, have the same parents and the same background, but they differ considerably in appearance and lifestyle.

Another way of writing an introduction is to begin with a very general idea and to narrow it down in the main idea sentence. The above introduction could also have been written in this way:

> Some brothers are as different as night and day. Both my brothers, Nick and Joe, have the same parents and the same background, but they differ considerably in appearance and lifestyle.

EXERCISE 10-B

Write an introduction for each of the three compositions in Exercise 10-A. Begin your introduction with a common belief or a general statement, as explained above. Then continue with the main idea sentence you have chosen.

1. _____

_____

_____

_____

_____

_____

2. _____

3. _____

Finding Similarities and Differences

It is important to examine carefully the two things you want to compare or contrast. The following exercise will give you practice in looking for similarities and differences.

140 BASIC COMPOSITION FOR ESL

EXERCISE 10-C

Look at the pictures below. The people or things pictured have similarities as well as differences. List at least three similarities and three differences for each pair of pictures.

Julie **Sandy**

20 YEARS OLD   20 YEARS OLD

1. *Similarities*

   1. *long hair*
   2. _____
   3. _____

Differences

   1. Julie: *thin face*
      Sandy: *round face*

   2. Julie: _____
      Sandy: _____

   3. Julie: _____
      Sandy: _____

COMPARING AND CONTRASTING **141**

Empire State Building

Eiffel Tower

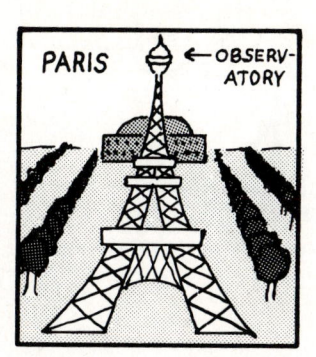

2. *Similarities*

   1. _____

   2. _____

   3. _____

Differences

   1. Empire State Bldg.: _____

      Eiffel Tower: _____

   2. Empire State Bldg.: _____

      Eiffel Tower: _____

   3. Empire State Bldg.: _____

      Eiffel Tower: _____

Tony's car

Sara's car

3. *Similarities*

   1. _____

   2. _____

   3. _____

Differences

   1. Tony's car: _____

      Sara's car: _____

   2. Tony's car: _____

      Sara's car: _____

   3. Tony's car: _____

      Sara's car: _____

COMPARING AND CONTRASTING **143**

Book 1   **Book 2**

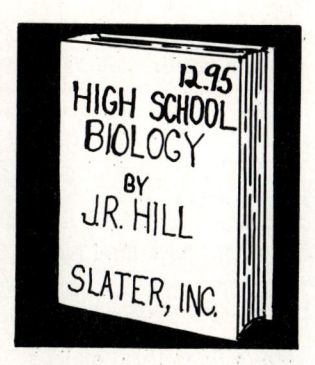

Book 1: 6.95 COLLEGE CHEMISTRY BY J.R. HILL SLATER, INC

Book 2: 12.95 HIGH SCHOOL BIOLOGY BY J.R. HILL SLATER, INC.

4. *Similarities*

   1. _____

   2. _____

   3. _____

Differences

   1. Book 1: _____

      Book 2: _____

   2. Book 1: _____

      Book 2: _____

   3. Book 1: _____

      Book 2: _____

Using *Both* for Similarities

When two things or people have something in common, we often use *both* to compare them. *Both* is grammatically plural, so it requires the plural verb form.

EXAMPLES

Julie has long hair. Sandy has long hair.

Both Julie and Sandy *(Both* of them) have long hair.

Julie and Sandy *both* (They *both)* have long hair.

When using a form of the verb *to be* in this type of sentence, *both* appears after the verb.

Julie and Sandy are *both* students.

EXERCISE 10-D

Write sentences using *both* for the similarities you found in the pictures in Exercise 10-C.

1. Both Julie and Sandy wear glasses.
   Julie and Sandy both wear glasses.

2.

3.

4.

5.

6.

7.

8.

Using *But* for Differences

When we want to show that two things are different or contrasting, we often use *but* to show the contrast. Notice the punctuation used with *but*.

EXAMPLES

Nick's hair is long, *but* Joe's is short.

Nick lives alone, *but* Joe lives with his family.

EXERCISE 10-E

Write sentences using *but* for the differences you found in the pictures in Exercise 10-C.

1. The Empire State Building is made of stone, but the Eiffel Tower is made of steel.

2.

3.

4.

5.

6.

7.

8.

Transitions Showing Contrast: *On the Other Hand*

Model Composition 10 has two major parts: the paragraph about Nick and the paragraph about Joe. A transition *(on the other hand)* is used to connect these two contrasting paragraphs. Underline this transition in the model composition.

On the other hand can also be used to show the contrast between two things or people in individual sentences.

EXAMPLES

Lily always dresses up. Her sister, *on the other hand,* usually wears blue jeans.

Gold is a precious and rare metal. *On the other hand,* iron is cheap and abundant.

EXERCISE 10-F

Use *on the other hand* to show the contrasting relationship in the following pairs of sentences.

1. Susan loves cats. Her husband hates them.

   Susan loves cats. Her husband, on the other hand, hates them.

2. The winters in New York City are cold and snowy. The summers are hot and humid.

3. Salomon speaks English very well. His wife speaks it poorly.

4. The University of Pennsylvania is located in an urban area. Pennsylvania State University is in a rural area.

5. Most of the earth's surface is covered by water. The surface of the moon is entirely dry.

6. In the United States, a nod means "yes." In Bulgaria, it means "no."

GRAMMAR AND PUNCTUATION

Comparatives

When we compare two things that are different, we often use the **comparative degree** of adjectives.

For one-syllable adjectives *(tall, thin, big)*, add *-er* to the adjective, and use *than* after the adjective. Double the final consonant if the adjective ends in a single consonant preceded by a single vowel *(big—bigger, fat—fatter)*.

>John is tall*er than* Nat (is).
>John is bigg*er than* Nat (is).

For two-syllable adjectives ending in *y (hap-py, la-zy)*, add *-er* to the adjective, and use *than* after it. Change *y* to *i* if a consonant precedes it.

>Mr. Rossi is happi*er than* Ms. Roter (is).
>She is angri*er than* he (is).

For most other two-syllable and all three-syllable adjectives, place *more* in front of the adjective and *than* after it.

>She seems *more* intelligent *than* he (does).
>That watch is *more* expensive *than* this one (is).

EXERCISE 10-G

Give the number of syllables in each of the following words. Then write the comparative form of each.

1. expensive   3   more expensive

2. easy

3. fast

4. crowded

5. friendly

6. thin

7. dirty

8. successful

9. happy

10. handsome

11. honest

12. hot

13. difficult

14. curly

15. clean

EXERCISE 10-H

Write one comparative sentence for each of the words in parentheses. Use a form of the verb *to be* in all of your sentences.

1. Alaska has an area of 589,757 square miles (1,527,469 square kilometers). Texas has an area of 267,338 square miles (692,405 square kilometers). *(big, small)*

    Alaska is bigger than Texas.
    Texas is smaller than Alaska.

2. The Sears Tower in Chicago is 1,454 feet (436 meters) tall. The World Trade Center in New York City is 1,353 feet (406 meters) tall. *(tall, short)*

3. Joan and Bill are both students at the university. Joan studies five hours a night. Bill studies only a few hours each weekend. *(lazy, industrious)*

4. Quibdo, Colombia, has an average rainfall of 345 inches (863 centimeters) a year. Bataques, Mexico, has an average annual rainfall of 1.2 inches (3 centimeters) per year. *(dry, wet)*

5. Bob weighs 120 pounds (54 kilograms), but his friend Rafael weighs 200 pounds (90 kilograms). *(light, heavy)*

6. A Volkswagen Rabbit can run 40 miles (64 kilometers) on a gallon of gas. A Cadillac, however, gets only 15 miles (24 kilometers) per gallon. *(cheap to operate, expensive to operate)*

7. Maria is 30 years old. Mohammed is 28. *(old, young)*

8. Houston, Texas, has an average temeprature of 53°F. (11.7°C.) in January. Chicago has an average temperature of 25°F. (—3.9°C.) in January. *(cold, warm)*

STUDENT OUTLINE 10
Two Sisters

Imagine you have met two very different women at a party. You are surprised later when you find out they are sisters. You discuss these differences in a letter to a friend. Use these pictures of Joyce and Karen in preparing to write about their differences. Use the outline of Model Composition 10 if you need a guide.

Helpful vocabulary: Joyce   Karen

                sweater   wear (suit, glasses)
                jeans   lawyer
                mechanic   go to the theater
                ride a bicycle   pets

Main idea sentence: _____

_____

_____

_____

_____

                              I. Joyce
                                   A.

154   BASIC COMPOSITION FOR ESL

B.

C.

D.

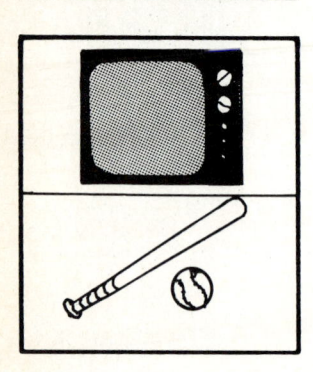

E.

F.

II. Karen
   A.

   B.

156 BASIC COMPOSITION FOR ESL

C.

D.

E.

F.

STUDENT COMPOSITION 10
Two Sisters

Stepping Along

Step 1: Use your outline to help you write a composition. In addition to your major paragraphs, write an introduction using your main idea sentence.

Step 2: Exchange your composition with a partner. As you read your partner's composition, think about these questions:
-Is everything in your partner's composition clear to you?
-Is paragraphing correct?
-Is a transition used to introduce the second major paragraph?
-Has your partner used the comparative form correctly? Underline lightly any uses of the comparative, and decide if the form is correct.
-Can you give your partner at least three suggestions for improvement?

Step 3: Talk with your partner about your compositions. Try to agree on improvements you can make.

Step 4: Rewrite your composition, making any changes you feel are necessary.

Further steps: As directed by your teacher.

MODEL COMPOSITION 11
Two Houses for Sale

Similarities

Differences

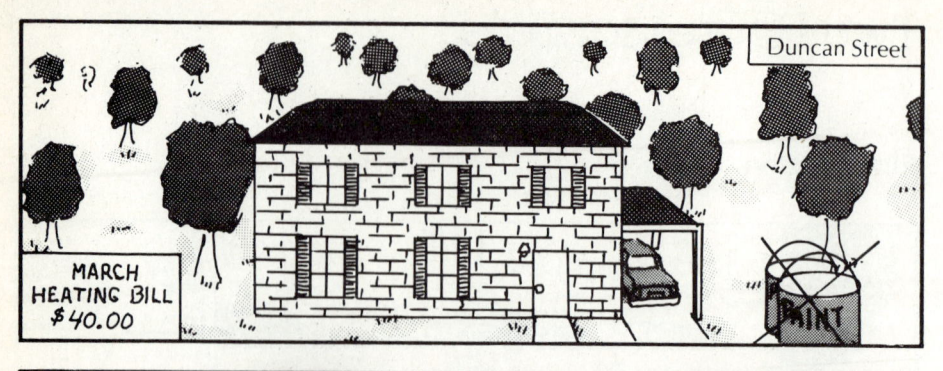

Purchasing a house requires careful observation. Century Realty has two houses for sale. They might at first seem similar; however, there are important differences between them.

One obvious similarity is their price. Both the house on Duncan and the one on Arla sell for $60,000. Their interiors are also practically the same. They both have two bedrooms, a large kitchen, a living room, a dining room, and a full bathroom. Neither house has a garage. Instead, each has a carport on one side.

The homes have important differences, however. The house on Duncan is built of brick, so it does not need much upkeep. The one on Arla, on the other hand, needs to be painted occasionally because it is made of wood. The brick house has a big backyard with many trees. The wooden house has no backyard. The most important difference is in their heating costs. The monthly heating bills of the residence on Arla are much higher.

The two houses for sale, then, share some similarities. However, because of the differences, the one on Duncan is a better value.

ORGANIZATION

Outlining

Model Composition 10 was organized into two major sections: the first paragraph was about Nick, and the second one about Joe. Model Composition 11 is organized differently. It balances the differences and similarities point by point. The following incomplete outline of the model composition shows this clearly. Can you complete the outline?

Outline of Model Composition 11

Introduction

I. Similarities
   A. Price
      1. House on Duncan: $60,000
      2. House on Arla: $60,000
   B. Interiors
      1. House on Duncan: 6 rooms
      2. House on Arla: 6 rooms
   C. Parking facilities
      1. House on Duncan: carport
      2. _____

II. Differences
   A. Construction materials
      1. House on Duncan: brick
      2. House on Arla: wood
   B. Yard
      1. _____
      2. House on Arla: no backyard
   C. _____
      1. House on Duncan: low
      2. House on Arla: high

Conclusion

EXERCISE 11-A Irrelevant Sentences

Read the following comparison/contrast paragraphs. Find the sentence in each one which does not support the main idea sentence. Cross it out.

1. Mosquitoes and houseflies differ in appearance and habits, but the two insects share many similarities. First, both are typical of hot, humid climates. Both insects suck their food. Houseflies suck their food from various sources, while most mosquitoes suck blood from animals and people. Both insects can cling to smooth surfaces and even walk upside down across ceilings. Finally, both can spread serious diseases. Houseflies spread typhoid, tuberculosis, and cholera, and mosquitoes carry malaria and yellow fever. Mosquitoes that carry malaria bite at night.

2. La Cuisine serves French food and Minutello's serves Italian food; however, the two restaurants have many things in common. Both their dining rooms are clean and elegant. Also, their meals are carefully prepared and reasonably priced. Italian food is as delicious as French food. In addition, the service is excellent at both restaurants. Their waiters are friendly and polite. Finally, both La Cuisine and Minutello's are open until very late at night.

3. Moths and butterflies are closely related and look very much alike; however, they differ from each other in four ways. First, most moths are active at night, but most butterflies are active during the day. Butterflies fly from flower to flower sucking their "nectar." Second, when moths rest, they spread their wings out. Butterflies, in contrast, hold their wings straight up. Their antennae are also different. The antennae of most moths are hairlike and pointed. All butterflies have knobs at the end of their antennae. Finally, the bodies of most moths are thick. The bodies of butterflies are thin.

GRAMMAR AND PUNCTUATION

Transitions Showing Contrast: *However*

However expresses contrast. It can connect two paragraphs or two sentences. Notice the punctuation used with the different positions of *however*. *However* is used mostly in formal writing.

EXAMPLE

Alaska is a large state; *however,* it has a small population.

Alaska is a large state. *However,* it has a small population.

Alaska is a large state. It has a small population, *however.*

EXERCISE 11-B

Underline all uses of *however* in Model Composition 11. Decide which ones connect sentences and which ones connect paragraphs.

EXERCISE 11-C

Connect the following sentences using *however.* Use all three positions and correct punctuation.

1. The food in the Broadway Cafe is excellent. The service is poor.

The food in the Broadway Cafe is excellent; however, the service is poor.

2. Athens is a very old city. It has many modern buildings.

3. It is warm outside. Our house is cold.

4. Chuck doesn't study much. He does well in school.

5. The New Jersey shore is crowded in the summer. Very few people go there in the winter.

6. The bite of a coral snake is nearly painless. It can cause death.

EXERCISE 11-D *However/But* Review

Decide which of the following pairs of sentences express contrast. Combine such sentences with *but* or *however*. Write *no* after the sentences that do not express contrast.

1. Ostriches have wings. They cannot fly.

2. We are going to buy a used car. We cannot afford a new one.

3. Thomas Edison was not a successful student. He became one of the most important inventors in history.

4. Smoking cigarettes is unhealthy. Many people smoke.

5. They were driving fast. They got a speeding ticket.

6. The spider looks very delicate. It can survive almost anywhere.

7. He went out to eat. Then he went to a movie.

8. The price is high. We are still going to buy the house.

9. The steamship *Titanic* sank. It struck an iceberg.

10. She doesn't like pizza. She ate some last night.

Using *Neither* for Similarities

You have learned that when two things or people have something in common we can use *both* to compare them. When two people or things have something negative in common we often use *neither*. In the following examples, *neither* is the subject of the sentence. It is grammatically singular and takes a singular verb.

EXAMPLES

The house on Arla does not have a garage.
The house on Duncan does not have a garage.

COMPARING AND CONTRASTING   **167**

Neither of the houses has a garage.

Neither house has a garage.

Note that *of the* can be dropped. The plural noun then becomes singular.

EXERCISE 11-E

Combine the information in the following pairs of sentences by using *neither*. Write each sentence two ways.

1. Mr. Schaeffer doesn't have a car.
   Mr. Jonescu doesn't have a car.

   Neither of the men has a car.

   Neither man has a car.

2. My sister Anne doesn't like disco music.
   My sister Karen doesn't like disco music.

   _____

   _____

3. The state of Hawaii is not part of the mainland of the United States.
   The state of Alaska is not part of the mainland of the United States.

   _____

   _____

4. The house on the corner is not for sale.
   The house across the street is not for sale.

   _____

   _____

5. The shoe store is not open on Sundays.
   The hardware store is not open on Sundays.

   _____

   _____

6. The planet Mercury does not have any satellites.
   The planet Venus does not have any satellites.

   _____

   _____

7. The history teacher doesn't live near the university.
   The biology teacher doesn't live near the university.

   _____

   _____

COMPARING AND CONTRASTING   **169**

EXERCISE 11-F *Neither/Both* Review

Use the picture to write sentences with *both* and *neither*.

Both

1. *Both Jack and Fred have bats.*

2.

3.

4.

Neither
5.

6.

7.

STUDENT OUTLINE 11
Two Apartments for Rent

Similarities

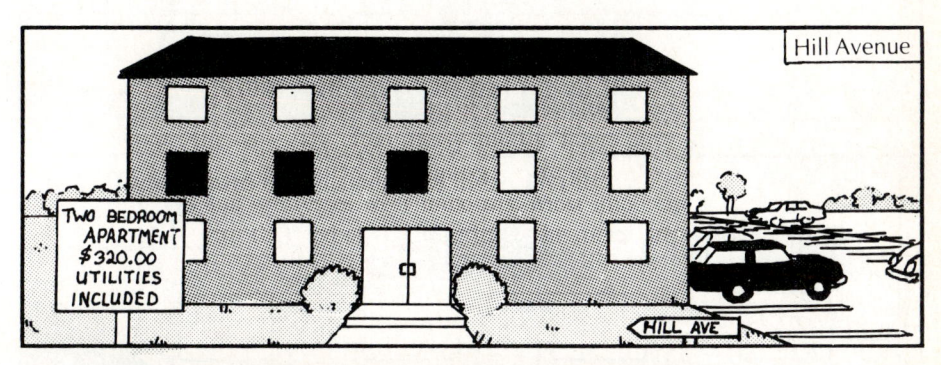

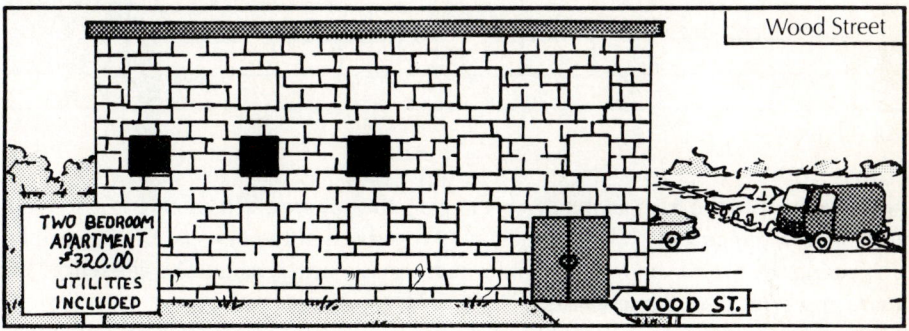

171

Differences

Imagine that a friend from another city is moving to your area. The friend has asked you to look at two rental apartments which were advertised in the newspaper. You will be comparing the two to show your friend which one is a better value. The differences are more important than the similarities, so you will emphasize these in your composition. Complete the outline; you should have at least three major points for each paragraph.

Helpful vocabulary: rent   dishwasher
                    second floor   basement
                    building   laundry facilities
                    parking lot   do the laundry
                    wall-to-wall carpeting   laundromat

Main idea sentence: _____
_____
_____
_____
_____
_____

I. Similarities

II. Differences

STUDENT COMPOSITION 11
Two Apartments for Rent

Stepping Along

Step 1: Use your outline to help you write a composition. In addition to your major paragraphs, write an introduction paragraph using your main idea sentence. Use *neither* at least once, and write appropriate transitions.

Step 2: Exchange your composition with a partner. As you read your partner's composition, think about these questions:
-Did your partner follow all the directions in Step 1?
-Is everything in your partner's composition clear to you?
-Can you give your partner at least three suggestions for improvement?

Step 3: Talk with your partner about your compositions. Try to agree on improvements you can make.

Step 4: Rewrite your composition, making any changes you feel are necessary.

Further steps: As directed by your teacher.

MODEL COMPOSITION 12
Two Cities

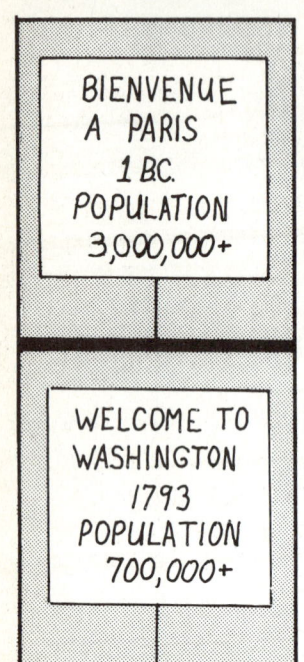

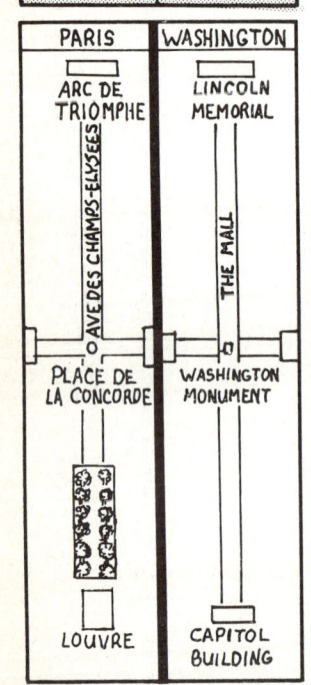

It is difficult to imagine that a large, old city and a new, small city could be similar at all. However, anyone who has seen Paris and Washington can tell that this is possible. The two cities differ in age and population, but they share many similarities.

Of course, Paris is much older than Washington. The French city is over 2,000 years old. Washington, in contrast, is very young. It is less than 200 years old. The population of Paris is also much larger than Washington's. Paris has more than 3,000,000 people. Washington has just over 700,000.

Although these important differences exist, the cities are strikingly similar. First, both cities are the political centers of their countries. The president of France lives in the heart of Paris, in the Elysée Palace. Likewise, the president of the United States lives in the heart of Washington, in the White House. The French National Assembly meets in Paris, in the Palais Bourbon. The Congress of the United States has its meeting place in Washington, in the Capitol Building. Second, the two cities look similar. L'Enfant, the French engineer who designed Washington, was greatly influenced by the layout of the capital of France. For this reason, many of the buildings and monuments in Washington are symmetrically located in view of one another, just as they are in Paris. Both cities are also the sites of magnificent monuments, important historical landmarks, fine museums, beautiful parks, and broad, tree-lined avenues. Finally, tourism is as important for Washington as it is for Paris. Every year, millions of tourists from all parts of the world visit these cities to view their attractions.

In conclusion, the cities of Paris and Washington share striking similarities. Both are political and tourist centers and have similar layouts.

ORGANIZATION

Outlining

The organization of Model Composition 12 is the same as the one for Model Composition 11. It follows a point-by-point sequence. Look carefully at the following incomplete outline of the model composition. Can you complete it?

Outline of Model Composition 12

Introduction

I. Differences
   A. Age
      1. Paris: over two thousand years old
      2. Washington: less than two hundred years old
   B. Population
      1. _____
      2. Washington: just over 700,000

II. _____
   A. Political centers
      1. Home of government leaders
         a. Paris: residence of president of France
         b. _____
      2. Home of government legislatures
         a. Paris: meeting place of the French National Assembly
         b. Washington: meeting place of Congress
   B. Layout
      1. Paris: symmetrical layout
      2. _____
   C. Points of interest
      1. Paris: monuments, historical landmarks, museums, parks, avenues
      2. Washington: monuments, historical landmarks, museums, parks, avenues
   D. _____
      1. Paris: millions of tourists
      2. Washington: millions of tourists

Conclusion

Transitions Showing Contrast and Similarity

You already know some of the transitions used to connect two contrasting sentences or paragraphs. *In contrast* is another transition you can use to show contrast. Note the punctuation used.

EXAMPLES

Paris is over 2,000 years old. Washington, *in contrast,* is very young.

Paris is over 2,000 years old. *In contrast,* Washington is very young.

There are also transitions that introduce similarities between two sentences or two paragraphs. Two of them are *likewise* (used in the model composition) and *similarly*. A comma is usually used after these transitions.

EXAMPLES

The president of France lives in the capital of France.

Likewise,
Similarly, the president of the U.S. lives in the capital of the U.S.

EXERCISE 12-A

The following is *not* a good composition because none of the sentences that introduce similarity or contrast contain transitions. Read the composition and decide which sentences could be improved by using transitions. Then rewrite the composition using *in contrast, on the other hand, however, likewise,* or *similarly* where appropriate.

     Hotels and motels are the most common kinds of accommodations for travelers in the United States. Although both provide housing and a variety of services, they do differ in some respects.
     Hotels and motels serve their guests in similar ways. Hotels, for instance, have restaurants and cafeterias. Many motels provide facilities for meals. In addition, hotels often have swimming pools, golf courses, or tennis courts. Many motels offer various recreational facilities.
     In spite of these similarities, hotels and motels are different. First, hotels are generally larger than motels; some have over thirty floors. Motels have only one or two floors. In addition, most hotels have ballrooms for conventions. Motels usually don't. Most hotels are located in downtown sections. Motels are found along highways, frequently at intersections or at exits to highways. Perhaps the main difference between hotels and motels is the room arrangement. In a hotel, you have to go through a lobby to reach your room. In a motel, you can drive your car up to the door of your room.
     Hotels and motels, then, provide a variety of similar services, but their size, location, and room arrangement are often different.

Rewritten composition

_____

_____

_____

_____

_____

_____

_____

_____

_____

Main Idea Sentences and Introductions

The following phrases will be useful to you when you are writing main idea sentences for comparison/contrast compositions.

X and Y have many things in common.
X and Y have few things in common.

X and Y are very similar.
X and Y are very different.

X and Y share many similarities.
X and Y have many differences.

X resembles Y.
X and Y differ.

X is similar to Y.
X is different from Y.

Remember that when you compare and contrast, your main idea sentence will contain two parts. Even if it has the two parts, however, it may not be suitable, as the following example shows.

Poor: The sculptors Michelangelo and Rodin are different; however, they have many things in common.

This main idea sentence tells 1) what is being compared, and 2) what will be emphasized. It does not give the reader any information, however, about *what* is similar or *what* is different between the two artists. Just saying that two things or people are "different but similar" or "similar but different" is not enough. The following example *is* an acceptable main idea sentence because it gives some introductory information on *what* is different between them (they lived in different centuries and different countries) and *what* is similar (their works of art).

Better: The sculptors Michelangelo and Rodin lived in different centuries and different countries; however, their works of art have many things in common.

In the above example, both parts of the main idea sentence are expanded, but it is often sufficient to expand only one part.

If you were writing a longer composition, you would expand this main idea sentence into an introduction. You could begin with a common belief and then show it is not true:

> Most people do not see many similarities between Michelangelo and Rodin. It is true that the sculptors lived in different centuries and different countries; however, their works of art have many things in common.

Or you might begin with a general statement:

> Michelangelo and Rodin are two of history's greatest sculptors. They lived in different centuries and different countries; however, their works of art have many things in common.

EXERCISE 12-B

Read each comparison/contrast composition carefully and write an introduction for it. Remember that an introduction must include a main idea sentence.

1. _____

_____

_____

_____

_____

Lions are large, fierce, powerful beasts which look very frightening. They are known as "kings of the jungle." Cats, on the other hand, are small, quiet, gentle animals which do not look threatening. They are completely domesticated.

However, both animals are members of the same family: the Felidae family. Both are covered with the same soft fur and have the same long whiskers on their face. Both the lion and the cat are meat-eating mammals. They are also well-coordinated; they can climb easily and usually land on their feet after a fall. They move quickly and quietly on soft, padded feet. Finally, both animals are very clean because they wash themselves frequently with their tongues.

2. _____

_____
_____
_____
_____
_____

    When eating, both Frenchmen and Americans enjoy table conversation. Both eat with knives and forks. Neither considers it polite to talk with food in the mouth.
    There are many differences in table manners, however. The French keep the fork in the left hand while eating meat; many Americans don't. In France, both hands should be kept on the table while eating. In the U.S., the left hand may be on the lap. Frenchmen break off a piece of bread with their fingers and eat it. Americans, in contrast, pick up the whole piece. Finally, Frenchmen eat fruit with a knife and fork. Americans usually use their fingers.

3. _____

_____
_____
_____
_____
_____

    Camels are large and have one or two humps on their backs. Llamas, in contrast, are small and have no humps. Camels live in the deserts of North Africa, Arabia, and Mongolia. Llamas live in South America.
    The two animals, however, have much in common. First, they belong to the same class of animals. They are hoofed, four-legged ruminants. Second, both can be bad tempered. Camels bite and kick when they get angry, and llamas spit at their enemy. Finally, both are commonly used in dry regions for transporting people or burdens because they can live for weeks without water. Their bodies retain water well because the animals sweat very little in the heat.

Conclusions

Compositions which are more than one paragraph in length usually need a short conclusion. The phrases *in conclusion* and *in summary* are sometimes used to begin a conclusion. A conclusion often restates the main idea sentence using different words. For example, in Model Composition 10, the main idea sentence states that although Nick and Joe are brothers, they are not similar. Notice how the conclusion restates the same idea using different words:

> My friends cannot believe that Nick and Joe are brothers because they seem so different.

In addition, a conclusion can summarize the major points of the composition. This summary may follow the restatement of the main idea sentence. In Model Composition 12, notice that the first sentence of the conclusion restates the main idea sentence. The second sentence summarizes the major points.

> In conclusion, the cities of Paris and Washington share striking similarities. Both are political and tourist centers and have similar layouts.

A conclusion can also make a judgment. Look at Model Composition 11. The conclusion includes a restatement (the first sentence) and a judgment (the second sentence).

> The two houses for sale, then, share some similarities. However, because of the differences, the one on Duncan is a better value.

EXERCISE 12-C

Write appropriate short conclusions for the compositions in Exercise 12-B.

1. _____

_____

_____

_____

_____

2. _____

3. _____

GRAMMAR AND PUNCTUATION

Comparing with *As...As*

When we compare two things that are the same, we often use *as . . . as*.

EXAMPLES

Sheila is *as tall as* Jack. (They are the same height.)
Mr. Kent is *as old as* Mr. James. (They are the same age.)

EXERCISE 12-D

Write a comparative sentence using the information given below and the words in parentheses. *Notice that your sentences will compare things that are different as well as things that are the same.* Use a form of the verb *to be* in all your sentences.

1. Norma and Helen are both 5 feet 8 inches (1.7 meters) tall. *(tall)*

   Norma is as tall as Helen.

2. Both the Golling Falls in Austria and the Agoyan Falls in Ecuador are two hundred feet high (60 meters). *(high)*

3. Mercury's diameter is 3,100 miles (4,960 kilometers). Jupiter's is 88,000 miles (140,800 kilometers). *(small)*

4. Both John and Donald can lift up to 250 pounds (90 kilograms). *(strong)*

5. In 1974 the tuition at Carnegie-Mellon University was $2,500. In the same year, the tuition at New York University was $2,700. *(expensive)*

6. One cup (240 milliliters) of skim milk has 9 grams of protein. One cup of whole milk also has 9 grams of protein. *(nutritious)*

7. Iris and Branka both weigh 130 pounds (58.5 kilograms). *(heavy)*

8. The Amazon River is 4,000 miles (6,400 kilometers) long. The Nile is 4,187 miles (6,699 kilometers) long. *(long)*

EXERCISE 12-E Review of Comparatives

Write two sentences comparing or contrasting each of the following pairs of things. Share your opinions with the class.

1. American food/food in your country

2. marijuana/alcohol

3. classical music/rock music

4. you/another member of your class

5. speaking English/writing English

6. solar energy/nuclear energy

7. a computer/a human brain

Showing Contrast with *Although*

Contrast can be shown by using *although* to introduce a dependent clause. The *although* clause can occur at the beginning of the sentence or at the end. Notice the difference in punctuation.

EXAMPLES

Although Manhattan is a very small island, it has a population of almost 1.5 million.

Manhattan has a population of almost 1.5 million *although it is a very small island.*

EXERCISE 12-F

In this exercise you will see two sentences which express a contrast. Combine the sentences by changing the italicized sentence to a clause beginning with *although*.

1. Violins and guitars have few things in common. *Their appearance is similar.*

   Violins and guitars have few things in common although their appearance is similar.

2. *Many people are afraid of thunder.* It is harmless.

3. No one knows how the Egyptian pyramids were built. *Experts have studied them for years.*

4. *To most of us, a tomato is a vegetable.* Botanists classify it as a fruit.

5. The population of the world is increasing. *The birth rate is falling.*

6. *The United States has tried to grow tea.* It has not succeeded.

EXERCISE 12-G

Fill in the blanks with an appropriate clause beginning with *although*.

1. _Although the tuition is high_, David will go to Harvard University.

2. They didn't turn on the air conditioner _____
   _____.

3. _____, no automobile accidents were reported.

4. She bought the car _____
   _____.

5. _____, I enjoyed myself at the picnic.

6. Although Sybil's health is poor, _____
   _____.

STUDENT OUTLINE AND COMPOSITION 12

Develop your own topic, or choose one of the following for your final comparison/contrast composition. Consider your fellow students as your audience.

1. Compare and contrast two cities or towns you know. Make your composition interesting and informative. If you want to discuss two cities or towns which are obviously different (for instance, a small town in India and a large city in the United States), it might be more interesting and informative to concentrate on the similarities. If you want to write about two cities or towns which are obviously similar (for instance, two neighboring towns on the Mediterranean), it might be more interesting to emphasize the differences.

2. Compare and contrast two members of your family. You might want to comment on some of the following points in your composition: physical appearances, personalities, attitudes and beliefs, jobs, leisure-time activities.

3. Compare and contrast yourself now with yourself five years ago. In what ways are you the same and in what ways are you different?

4. *CHALLENGER:* Now that you are familiar with the American college educational system, compare and contrast it with your own. In your composition, you might discuss the behavior of teachers, the behavior of students, the classroom arrangement, and homework or tests in the two countries.

Stepping Along

Step 1: After choosing your topic, take time to think and write an outline of your major points and additional details. You may organize your material as in Model Composition 10 or as in Model Composition 11 or 12.

Step 2: Form groups of about 3 students. Take turns explaining your outlines to each other. Stop each other and ask questions when you think something is not clear. Tell each other where you are interested in knowing additional details. (Remember that details help make your writing interesting.)

Step 3: Use your outline and your partners' suggestions to write your composition. Remember to use the following words to show **similarity:** *likewise, similarly, both, neither,* and *as . . . as.* Use these to show **difference:** *but, however, although, in contrast, on the other hand,* and *more/. . .er than.*

Step 4: When you finish writing, exchange compositions with a partner. As you read your partner's composition, think about these questions:
-Is there anything in the composition that is not clear to you?
-Is there enough detail to make the composition interesting?
-Did your partner use separate paragraphs for the introduction and conclusion?
-Does the introduction prepare you for what you will read?
-Lightly underline the words that show similarity and difference. (See Step 3). Does your partner use these correctly?
-Can you give your partner any suggestions for improvement?

Step 5: Talk with your partner about these questions and make suggestions for improvement.

Step 6: Rewrite your composition, making any changes you feel are necessary.

Further steps: As directed by your teacher.

UNIT FIVE
Classifying

INTRODUCTION

In this unit, you will learn how to classify. **Classifying** is another way to organize your thoughts and your writing. When we want to explain the relationship between *two* things, we compare and contrast them. When we want to explain the relationship among *a number* of things, we classify them. Things with similar characteristics are grouped together in this kind of organization.

Suppose you want to explain the American car market to your friend who is interested in buying an American car but knows little about what is available. You might start out by dividing cars into groups and making a chart as follows:

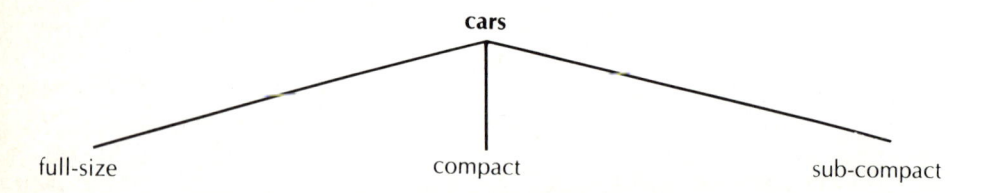

```
                        cars
              /          |          \
        full-size     compact     sub-compact
```

You could continue your explanation by giving examples for each group as follows:

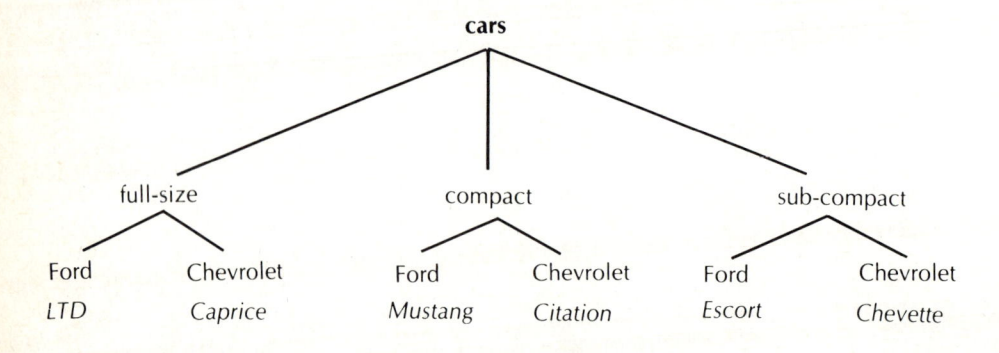

```
                            cars
              /              |              \
        full-size         compact        sub-compact
         /    \            /    \           /    \
      Ford  Chevrolet   Ford  Chevrolet   Ford  Chevrolet
      LTD   Caprice    Mustang Citation   Escort Chevette
```

As you make the chart, you are moving from **general** words to more **specific** words. The Ford *LTD* and the Chevrolet *Caprice* are part of the class of full-size cars. Full-size cars are part of the class of cars. Moving horizontally across the chart, we see items that are **parallel.** For instance, the items *full-size cars, compact cars,* and *subcompact cars* are similar in content and form. So are the items *Ford LTD, Chevrolet Caprice, Ford Escort, Chevrolet Citation, Ford Mustang,* and *Chevrolet Chevette.* These are important concepts to understand when classifying. This type of chart will help you organize your thoughts before writing.

How we classify depends, of course, on what we want to say. In the above chart, cars are classified according to their size. They could also be classified in many other ways, including according to cost, as in the following chart.

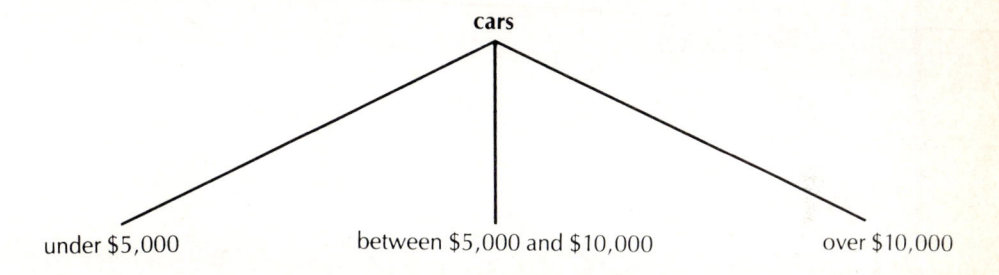

```
                          cars
           ╱               │               ╲
   under $5,000   between $5,000 and $10,000   over $10,000
```

Can you think of other useful ways to classify cars?

Classification is a form of organization used in all fields when people want to understand something better or explain it to someone else. A metallurgist, for example, might find it useful to explain the properties of various metals by classifying them, and someone in the medical field might want to classify various diseases to clarify the relationship among them. What could you explain by classification in your field of interest?

MODEL COMPOSITION 13
Amount of Carbohydrate in Foods

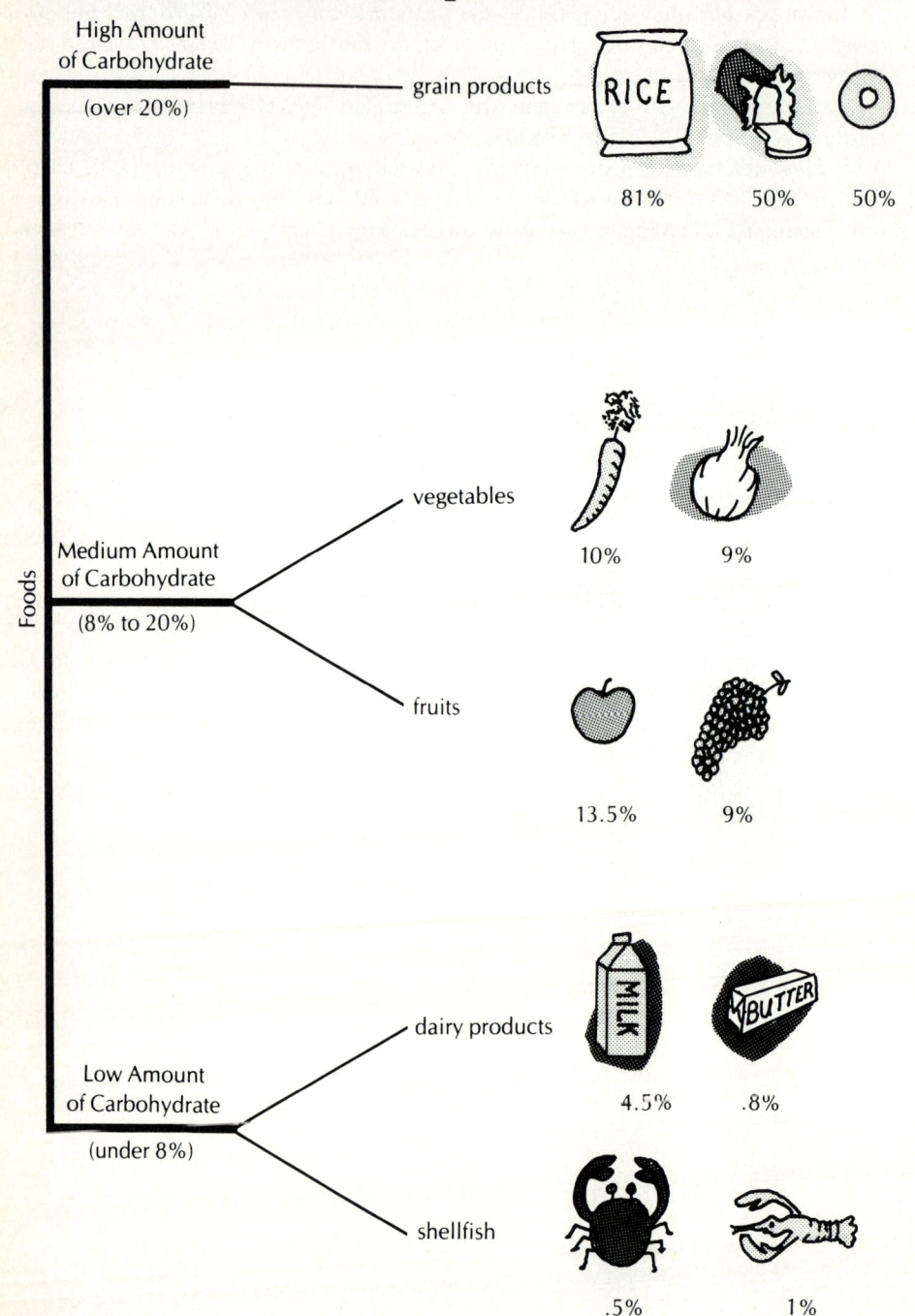

Foods
- High Amount of Carbohydrate (over 20%)
  - grain products
    - RICE 81%
    - 50%
    - 50%
- Medium Amount of Carbohydrate (8% to 20%)
  - vegetables
    - 10%
    - 9%
  - fruits
    - 13.5%
    - 9%
- Low Amount of Carbohydrate (under 8%)
  - dairy products
    - MILK 4.5%
    - BUTTER .8%
  - shellfish
    - .5%
    - 1%

Carbohydrate is the body's main source of energy. Many different foods contain this nutrient. These foods can be classified into a high, medium, or low group according to their carbohydrate content.

Most grain products are high in carbohydrates, so they belong in the high group. Rice, for instance, is composed of 81% carbohydrate. Both bread and doughnuts contain 50%.

Vegetables belong in the medium group. Carrots, for example, are composed of 10% carbohydrate, and onions contain 9%. Fruits are also in the medium group. Apples, for instance, are made up of 13.5% carbohydrate, and grapes contain 9%.

There are two categories of food in the low carbohydrate group: shellfish and dairy products. Lobster and crab are examples from the shellfish category. Lobster has only .5% carbohydrate, and crab has 1%. Milk, a member of the dairy products category, contains 4.5% carbohydrate. Butter, another dairy product, has only .8%

In summary, carbohydrate can be obtained from foods such as grain products, vegetables, fruit, dairy products, and shellfish. It is easy, therefore, to include sources of this essential nutrient in our diet.

ORGANIZATION

Outlining

The following outline shows the organization of the model composition. How many major pargraphs are in the composition?

Outline of Model Composition 13

Introduction
I. High group—grain products
    1. Rice: 81%
    2. Bread: 50%
    3. Doughnuts: 50%
II. Medium group
    A. Vegetables
        1. Carrots: 10%
        2. Onions: 9%
    B. Fruits
        1. Apples: 13.5%
        2. Grapes: 9%

III. Low group
   A. Shellfish
      1. Lobster: .5%
      2. Crab: 1%
   B. Dairy products
      1. Milk: 4.5%
      2. Butter: .8%

Conclusion

Classification Charts

Before you write, you should, of course, organize your material. When you want to explain something by classifying, you can use an outline or a **classification chart**. Remember that a classification chart should move from general (at the top) to specific (at the bottom). The words placed next to each other should be parallel (equal in form and content).

EXAMPLES

Look back at the unit introduction for examples of classification charts.

EXERCISE 13-A

Find appropriate words to fill the empty boxes in the following charts.

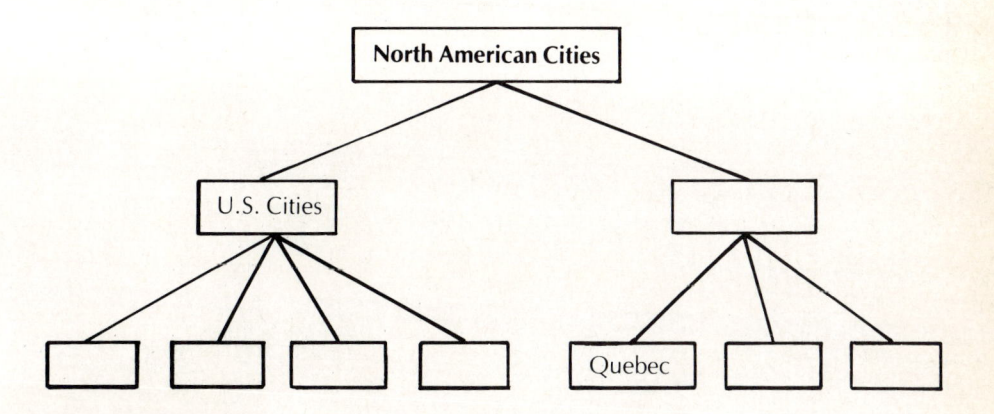

```
                    North American Cities
                   /                    \
            U.S. Cities                 [    ]
           / /  \  \                   / | \
         [ ][ ][ ][ ]              Quebec [ ] [ ]
```

BASIC COMPOSITION FOR ESL

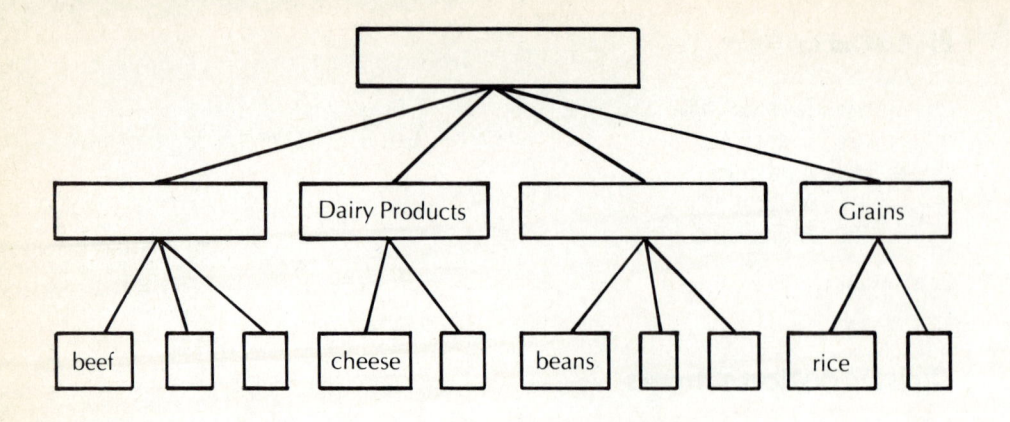

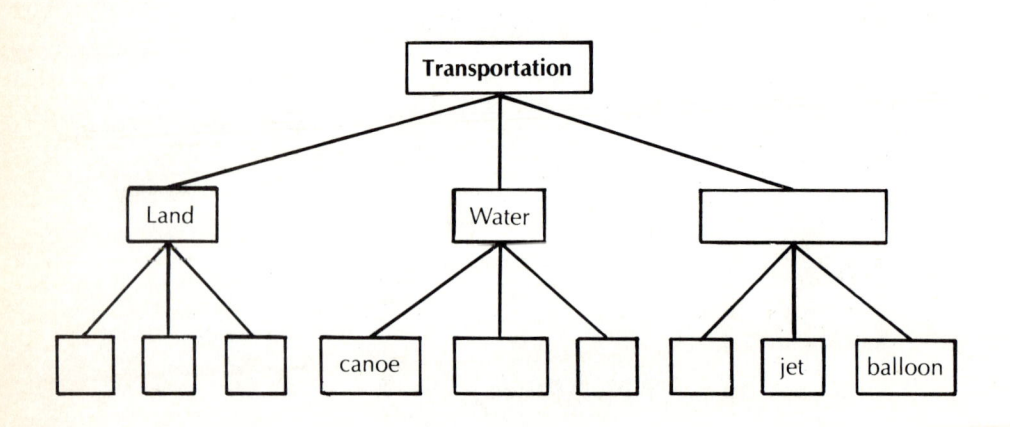

```
                    [                    ]
         /        /         \          \
     [      ]  Dairy Products  [     ]  Grains
     / | \      / | \        / | \    / | \
   beef       cheese        beans    rice
```

```
              Transportation
           /        |        \
        Land      Water      [     ]
       / | \      / | \      / | \
              canoe              jet  balloon
```

EXERCISE 13-B

Change the above classification charts to outlines. The word at the top of the chart is your topic. Remember to move from general to specific. The first outline has been started for you.

Topic 1:   North American cities

      I. U.S. cities

          A.

          B.

          C.

          D.

      II.

          A. Quebec

          B.

          C.

Topic 2:

Topic 3:

EXERCISE 13-C More Practice with General and Specific

In the following groups of words, one word is more specific or more general than the other words in the group. Find this word and cross it out. Then write *too specific* or *too general* in the answer blank.

1. football

    baseball

    ~~sport~~   *too general*

    tennis

2. furniture

    sofa

    chair

    table   _____

3. dress

    coat

    clothes

    pants   _____

4. fruit juices

    vodka

    alcoholic beverages

    soft drinks   _____

5. vegetables

    fruit

    meat

    beans   _____

6. appliance

    dishwasher

    television

    vacuum cleaner   _____

Main Idea Sentences and Introductions

When you classify, your main idea sentence should tell the reader 1) *what* you are going to classify, and 2) *how* you will divide the suject. This will include at least one of the following:

   a. Number of groups
   b. Name of groups
   c. Principle of division

EXAMPLES

⌐¹⌐   ⌐——2a——⌐ ⌐——2c——⌐
Cars can be classified into *three major groups according to size.*

⌐¹⌐   ⌐——2a——⌐ ⌐———— 2b ————⌐
Cars can be classified into *three major groups: full-size, compact, and sub-compact.*

⌐¹⌐   ⌐2a⌐ ⌐ 2c ⌐
Horses have *five major uses* in the United States.

EXERCISE 13-D

Choose the best main idea sentence for each of the following compositions.

1. Most importantly, dogs are pets and friends to millions of Americans. Many breeds make excellent playmates for children. Dogs make good companions and can brighten the life of an older person who lives alone.

    Dogs are also widely used in hunting. Some can smell the air and locate game birds; they then guide the hunter to the proper location. Bloodhounds follow scents on the ground, and retrievers pick up birds that have been shot and bring them back to the hunter.

In addition, dogs may serve as protection. They can be trained to guard their masters' homes and bark fiercely when someone tries to enter. They also help to awaken people in case of fire at night. Some dogs, known as seeing-eye dogs, can be trained to help and protect the blind.

a. There are many different kinds of dogs in the United States.
b. Dogs have at least three major uses in American society.
c. Dogs are very popular in the United States.

2.   Northern Chinese food is light and delicate. The staple food is wheat flour, which is used to make noodle dishes, steamed bread, and dumplings. Typical dishes from this area are barbequed meat and hot pot. The most famous northern delicacy is Peking duck.

Coastal food contains a lot of sugar and soy sauce. These are used to flavor stews, seafood, and vegetables. A well-known dish from this area is Bird's-Nest soup.

The food from the inland area is very spicy. Small red chilies or Szechwan peppers are used liberally for seasoning and make the food taste very hot. Characteristic dishes are Szechwan Beef and Kang Pao Chicken.

The least greasy food is found in the southern area. Here, much of the food is stir-fried, and a lighter soy sauce is used than in the coastal area. Southern dishes are often the most costly to prepare because highly concentrated chicken broth is used. Shark's Fin soup and egg rolls are typical examples of southern dishes.

a. There are many excellent Chinese dishes, including Peking duck, Bird's-Nest soup, and Kang Pao Chicken.
b. Chinese food can be classified according to its nutritional value.
c. Chinese food can be classified into four types: northern, coastal, inland, and southern.

3.   The executive branch of the government consists of the Executive Office of the president, the executive departments, and the independent agencies. The president is the chief executive and is elected by the people. The executive departments, such as State, Treasury, Defense, and Labor, conduct the administration of the national government. The independent agencies deal with areas such as aeronautics and space and interstate commerce.

The legislative branch consists of the Congress and five administrative agencies. Congress is divided into the Senate and the House of Representatives. The Senate has 100 senators, two from every state. The population of each state determines how many representatives it has in the House of Representatives.

The judicial branch includes the entire federal court system. These courts decide cases that involve the Constitution and federal laws. The highest court in the United States is the Supreme Court. The president appoints its justices, who hold office for life.

a. The United States government is divided into three branches: the executive, the legislative, and the judicial.
b. The United States government includes the president, the executive departments, the Congress, and the Supreme Court.
c. The executive, the legislative, and the judicial branches are the three major parts of the government.

EXERCISE 13-E

Write an introduction for each of the three compositions in Exercise 13-D. Begin your introduction with a common belief or general statement. Then continue with the main idea sentence you have chosen.

1. _____

_____

_____

_____

_____

_____

2. _____

_____

_____

_____

_____

_____

3. _____

_____

_____

_____

_____

_____

_____

Transitions for Giving Examples

When you classify, you divide your subject into groups or categories. For each category you mention, you should give examples. Your writing will be easier to understand if you use transitions to introduce your examples. The first example you give may be introduced by *for example* or *for instance*. Further examples may be introduced by *also* or *another*, both of which indicate addition.

EXERCISE 13-F

Look back at Model Composition 13. Circle examples of the above transitions. Notice how each is used.

EXERCISE 13-G

The following is the introduction and the first paragraph of a composition that classifies recent American films. Fill in the blanks with appropriate transitions.

The American film industry is constantly releasing new films on a variety of subjects. Most of these films, however, can be divided into six general categories.

Science fiction films are one popular type of film. *Star Wars,* _____, tells a futuristic tale about a civil war between planets in an imaginary galaxy. *2001: A Space Odyssey* is _____ a science fiction film. It is about two astronauts and a computer on a space voyage to Jupiter.

_____ well-known science fiction film is *Close Encounters of the Third Kind.* In this film, aliens from outer space come down to earth and appear to earthlings.

EXERCISE 13-H

Put the following information in paragraph form. Use appropriate transitions. Your paragraph will be the second paragraph of the above composition.

Disaster films, especially popular in the 1970s, are a second type of American film.
Jaws is a 1970s disaster movie that tells the story of a shark that repeatedly attacks people.
A popular film of this decade, *Earthquake,* shows the city of Los Angeles being destroyed by an earthquake.
Towering Inferno is a disaster film. In this movie, a fire breaks out in a skyscraper, and many people are burned to death or die by jumping out of windows.

GRAMMAR AND PUNCTUATION

Punctuation: The Colon

A **colon** *(:)* is often used to introduce a list or series of items. The part of the sentence *after* the colon explains or gives details about what appears in the part of the sentence *before* the colon. When the word in front of the series is a verb or a preposition, a colon is not needed. However, if the word in front of the series is a noun, you must use the colon.

EXAMPLES

Colon needed: They visited four *cities:* New York, London, Paris, and Istanbul.

No colon needed: They visited New York, London, Paris, and Istanbul.

Colon needed: There are two categories of food in the low-carbohydrate *group:* shellfish and dairy products.

No colon needed: The two categories of food in the low-carbohydrate group are shellfish and dairy products.

EXERCISE 13-I

Put a colon where appropriate in the following sentences. Some sentences need no colon.

1. The arts can be divided into three groups: performing arts, visual arts, and literature.
2. The four national languages in Switzerland are German, French, Italian, and Romansch.
3. The human nervous system has three main divisions: the central nervous system, the peripheral nervous system, and the autonomic nervous system.
4. Books can be classified into two groups: fiction and nonfiction.
5. To play baseball, you need a bat, a baseball, and a glove.
6. New York has five boroughs: Manhattan, Queens, Brooklyn, the Bronx, and Richmond.
7. John applied to four schools: the University of Michigan, Columbia University, the University of Pennsylvania, and the University of Colorado.
8. The blood of all higher animals consists of plasma, red blood cells, white blood cells, and blood platelets.
9. The flight departure times will be 8:15, 9:20, 11:45, and 6:15.
10. There are five principal types of dams: earth dams, rock-fill dams, gravity dams, arch dams, and buttress dams.
11. Yugoslavia has six republics: Slovenia, Croatia, Serbia, Bosnia-Hercegovina, Montenegro, and Macedonia.
12. A snow skier needs the following equipment: skis, boots, and poles.

STUDENT OUTLINE 13
Amount of Protein in Foods

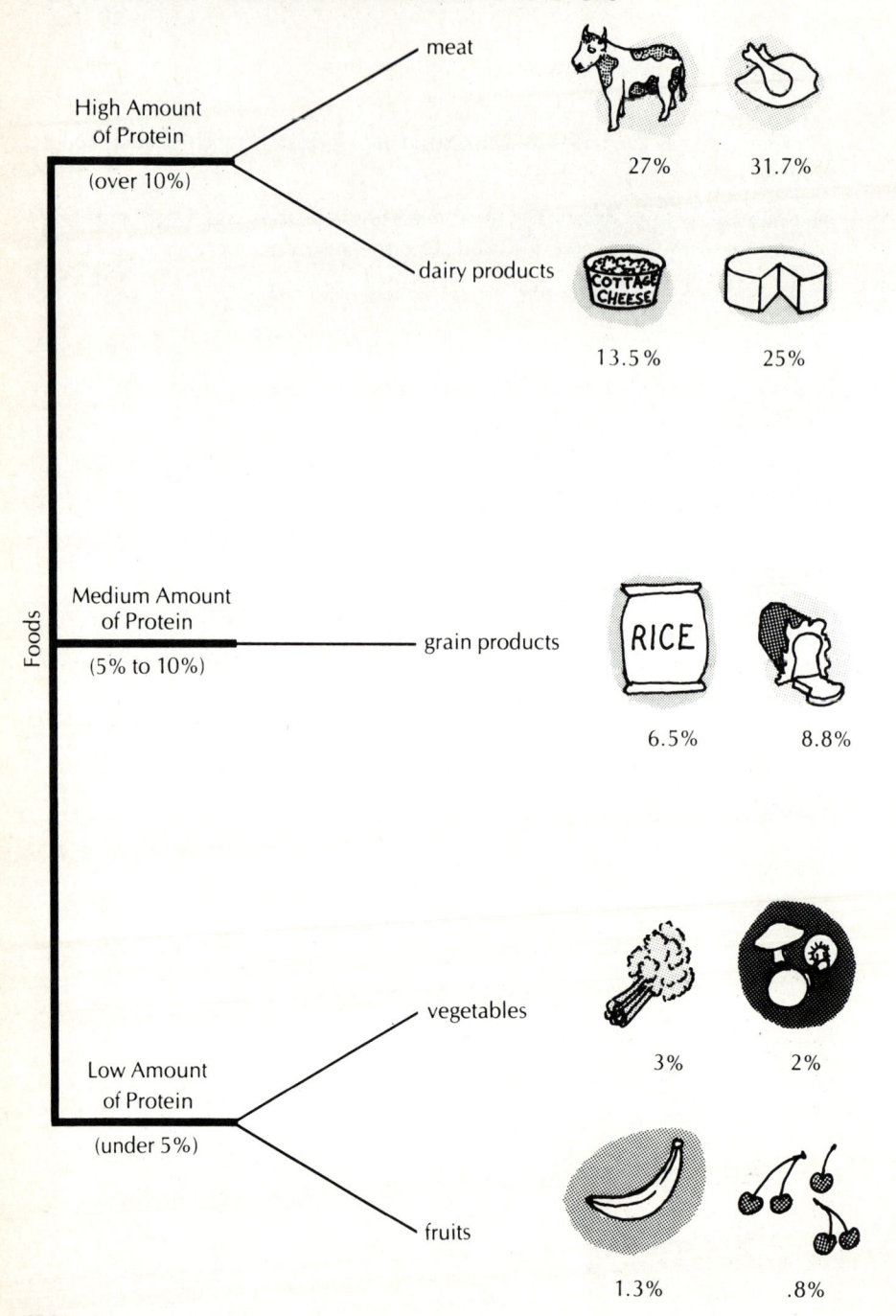

Foods
- High Amount of Protein (over 10%)
  - meat
    - 27%
    - 31.7%
  - dairy products
    - 13.5%
    - 25%
- Medium Amount of Protein (5% to 10%)
  - grain products
    - 6.5%
    - 8.8%
- Low Amount of Protein (under 5%)
  - vegetables
    - 3%
    - 2%
  - fruits
    - 1.3%
    - .8%

Suppose that you work for a health organization, which has asked you to classify and explain sources of protein in a handbook for the general public. Use this chart to help you write an outline and an introduction. Look at the chart carefully. How many major paragraphs will you have in your composition?

    Helpful vocabulary: beef
                                         chicken
                                         cottage cheese
                                         cheese
                                         broccoli
                                         mushrooms
                                         bananas
                                         cherries
                                        *contain
                                        *have
                                        *be composed of
                                        *be made up of

*Note: These verbs can be used as synonyms for each other. That is, they are different ways of saying the same thing.

Main idea sentence: _____

_____

_____

_____

_____

_____

Outline:

STUDENT COMPOSITION 13
Amount of Protein in Foods

Stepping Along

Step 1: Use your outline to help you write a composition. In addition to your major paragraphs, write an introduction paragraph using your main idea sentence and a conclusion. Use appropriate transitions.

Step 2: Exchange your composition with a partner. As you read your partner's composition, think about these questions:
-Has your partner used the correct number of paragraphs?
-Does your partner state the general topic at the beginning of the paragraph and then move to specific details?
-Has your partner used transitions to introduce some of the examples?
-Can you give your partner any suggestions for improvement?

Step 3: Talk with your partner about your compositions. Try to agree on improvements you can make.

Step 4: Rewrite your composition, making any changes you feel are necessary.

Further steps: As directed by your teacher.

MODEL COMPOSITION 14
Contact Sports

Contact Sports
- Team
  - Football
  - Ice Hockey
- Individual
  - Boxing
  - Fencing

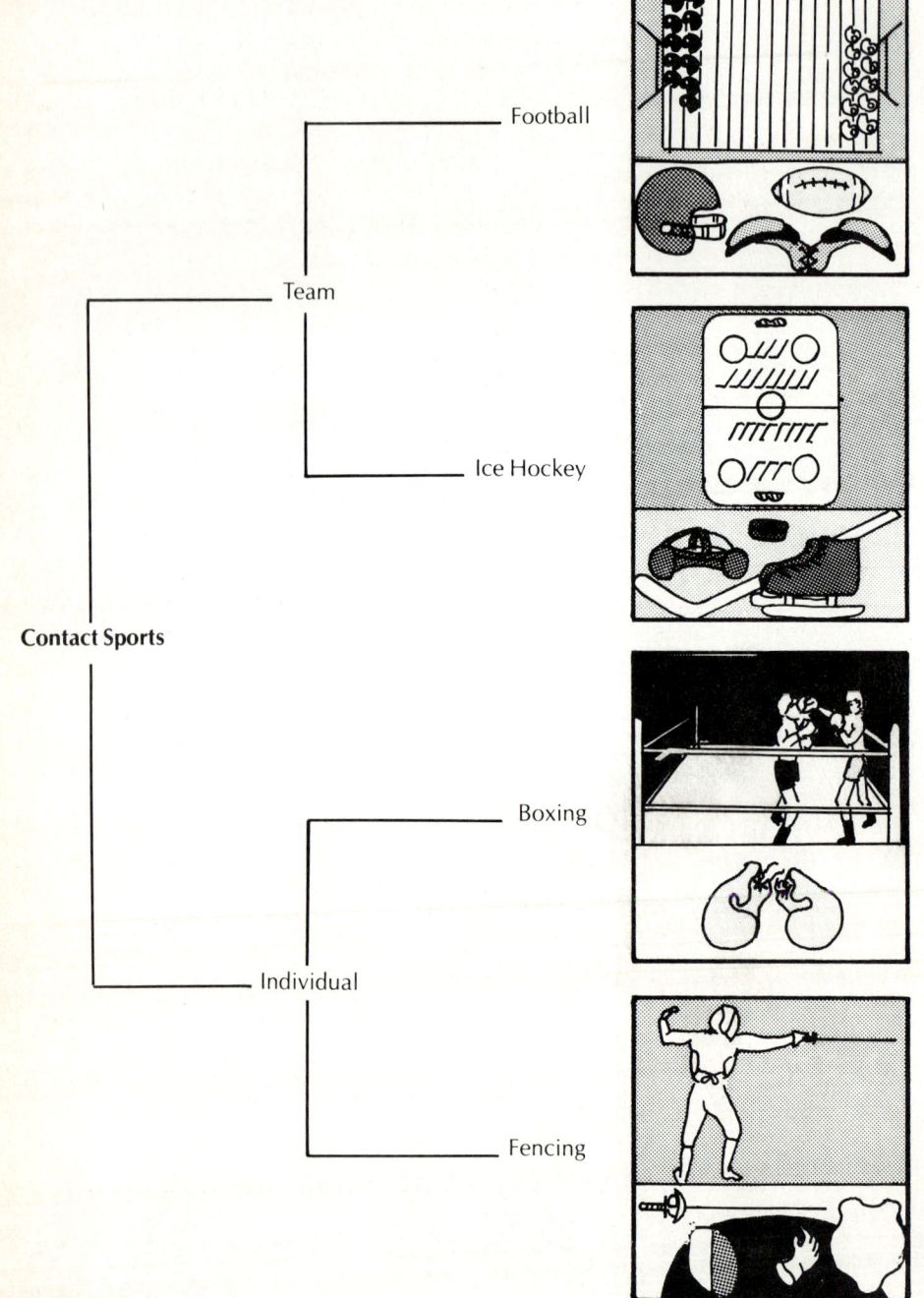

214

CLASSIFYING 215

Many sports require physical contact between opponents as a part of the play. These contact sports can be divided into two groups: team and individual.

One of the most popular team contact sports is football. There are eleven players on each team, and the game is played outside on a field called a gridiron. The players wear helmets and shoulder pads to protect themselves and use an oval leather ball called a football. Another popular team contact sport is ice hockey. Each team has six players. The game is played inside or outside on an ice-covered rink. Hockey players wear ice skates and helmets and use a curved stick to hit a rubber disk called a puck.

There are a number of individual contact sports. One is boxing. Boxing matches are held in a boxing ring, a padded area surrounded by ropes. Boxers use thick leather gloves to hit their opponents. Fencing is also an individual contact sport. It requires no special location. Fencers use a sword called a foil and wear heavy clothing and a mask.

In summary, contact sports are of two types. There are team contact sports, such as football and ice hockey, or individual contact sports, such as boxing and fencing.

ORGANIZATION

Outlining

The following incomplete outline shows the organization of the model composition. Can you complete it? How many major points does each paragraph have? How many additional details does each major point have?

Outline of Model Composition 14

Introduction

I. Team Contact Sports
   A. Football
      1. Number of players: eleven on each team
      2. Location: a gridiron
      3. Equipment: helmets, shoulder pads, football
   B. *Ice Hockey*
      1. Number of players: six on each team
      2. *Location: ice covered rink*
      3. *Equipment: skates, helmets, curved stick, puck*

II. *Individual Contact Sports*
   A. Boxing
      1. Location: boxing ring
      2. Equipment: boxing gloves

B. _____Fencing_____
   1. Location: no special location required
   2. _Equipment: foil, heavy clothing, mask_

Conclusion

EXERCISE 14-A Classification Outlines

Organize the following lists of words into outlines. The first one has been done for you.

1. Oak tree   I. Plants
   Minerals   A. Oak tree
   Dogs   B. Fern
   Camels   II. Minerals
   Fern   A. Iron
   Iron   B. Gold
   Gold   III. Animals
   Plants   A. Camels
   Animals   B. Dogs

2. South America
   Switzerland
   Ethiopia
   Africa
   France
   United States
   North America
   Nigeria
   Europe
   Kenya
   Germany
   Argentina
   Bolivia
   Canada
   Chile

3. Duck
   Beef
   Fish
   Chicken
   Poultry
   Tuna
   Lamb
   Swordfish
   Pork
   Oyster
   Meat
   Turkey

EXERCISE 14-B Irrelevant Sentences

Find the irrelevant sentence in each of the following classification paragraphs and cross it out.

1. Gardeners classify flowering plants into three groups: annuals, biennials, and perennials. Annuals normally live only one year. Examples of annuals are cornflowers and marigolds. It is expensive to use annuals in your garden because you must replace them every year. Biennials live for two years after the seeds are planted and bloom well only in the second year. Common biennials are foxgloves and hollyhocks. Perennials may live for many years. The flowers begin blooming the year after they are planted. Perennials include roses and violets.

2. The field of engineering can be divided into several different areas. Civil engineering is the branch that involves the construction of roads, bridges, railroads, and canals. Canals vary in length and width. Mechanical engineering deals with the designs and materials which are used in the construction of various kinds of machinery. Electrical engineering deals with the generation and transmission of electrical energy. Other areas of engineering include chemical, aeronautical, and military engineering.

3.   There are three types of gliders: the primary glider, the utility glider, and the sailplane. The primary glider has an open body, so the pilot has no protection. It is used for coasting downhill. The utility glider, which has an enclosed body, gives the occupants good protection. It is used for training in soaring and gliding. The sailplane has a slender body. It makes the best use of air currents and is used for soaring. The first World Championship Soaring Competition was held in Sweden in 1950.

GRAMMAR AND PUNCTUATION

Passive Sentences

All the sentences you have written so far in this text have been **active sentences.** An active sentence is a sentence in which the **agent** (that is, the one who performs the action) is in subject position. Sometimes, we do not know who the agent is, or we do not think that the agent is particularly important. We can then write a **passive sentence** by moving the agent out of the subject position and making the **receiver** the subject.

Active sentences in the present tense can be changed to passive sentences by making the receiver the subject and by using the present form of *to be* + *a past participle*. Note the following examples.

EXAMPLES

1a. *Active:*   Someone repairs *the roads* every year.

1b. *Passive:* *The roads* are repaired every year.

2a. *Active:*   Americans play *baseball* in the summer.

2b. *Passive:* *Baseball* is played (by Americans) in the summer.

In sentence 1b, the agent *(someone)* has been omitted because it is unknown or unimportant. In sentence 2b, the agent *(Americans)* may or may not be included, depending on its importance.

EXERCISE 14-C

Change the following active sentences to passive sentences. If the subject of the active sentence is *someone* or *people*, drop it when changing to the passive.

1. Golfers use clubs.

    Clubs are used by golfers.

2. People all over the world study English.

3. People play tennis and volleyball on courts.

4. Few Americans speak Arabic.

5. People make paper from wood.

6. People buy medicines at the drugstore.

7. The government collects taxes every year.

8. The landlord furnishes the apartment.

9. Someone serves lunch at noon.

10. Someone cleans the rooms once a week.

11. A mechanic on Green Street fixes my car.

12. Someone delivers the mail in the afternoon.

EXERCISE 14-D Punctuation: Review of the Colon

Summarize the information in the following sentences by organizing it into one sentence with a colon. Don't forget to use commas between items.

CLASSIFYING   **221**

1. To wash and wax a car, you need several things. First, you need a bucket of water, a sponge, and some mild detergent. After you wash the car, you need some wax and a soft cloth.

   To wash and wax a car you need several things: a bucket of water, a sponge, some mild detergent, some wax, and a soft cloth.

2. Sam visited several countries on his vacation. First, he toured Spain. Then he went to France and Germany. He also stopped in England and went through Nova Scotia on his way home.

3. Frank bought a lot of ingredients for his casserole. He bought noodles and a can of tomato sauce. He also bought mozzarella cheese and a pound of ground beef.

4. The new movie will be shown at the theater at various times. You can see it in the afternoon at 3:15 and 5:15. If you want to go at night, you can see the movie at 7:15 and 9:15.

5. Juanita is considering several possibilities for a career. She likes law. She is also interested in medicine. In addition, she is considering teaching.

STUDENT OUTLINE 14
Noncontact Sports

Noncontact Sports
- Team
  - Volleyball
  - Bobsledding
- Individual
  - Golf
  - Snow Skiing

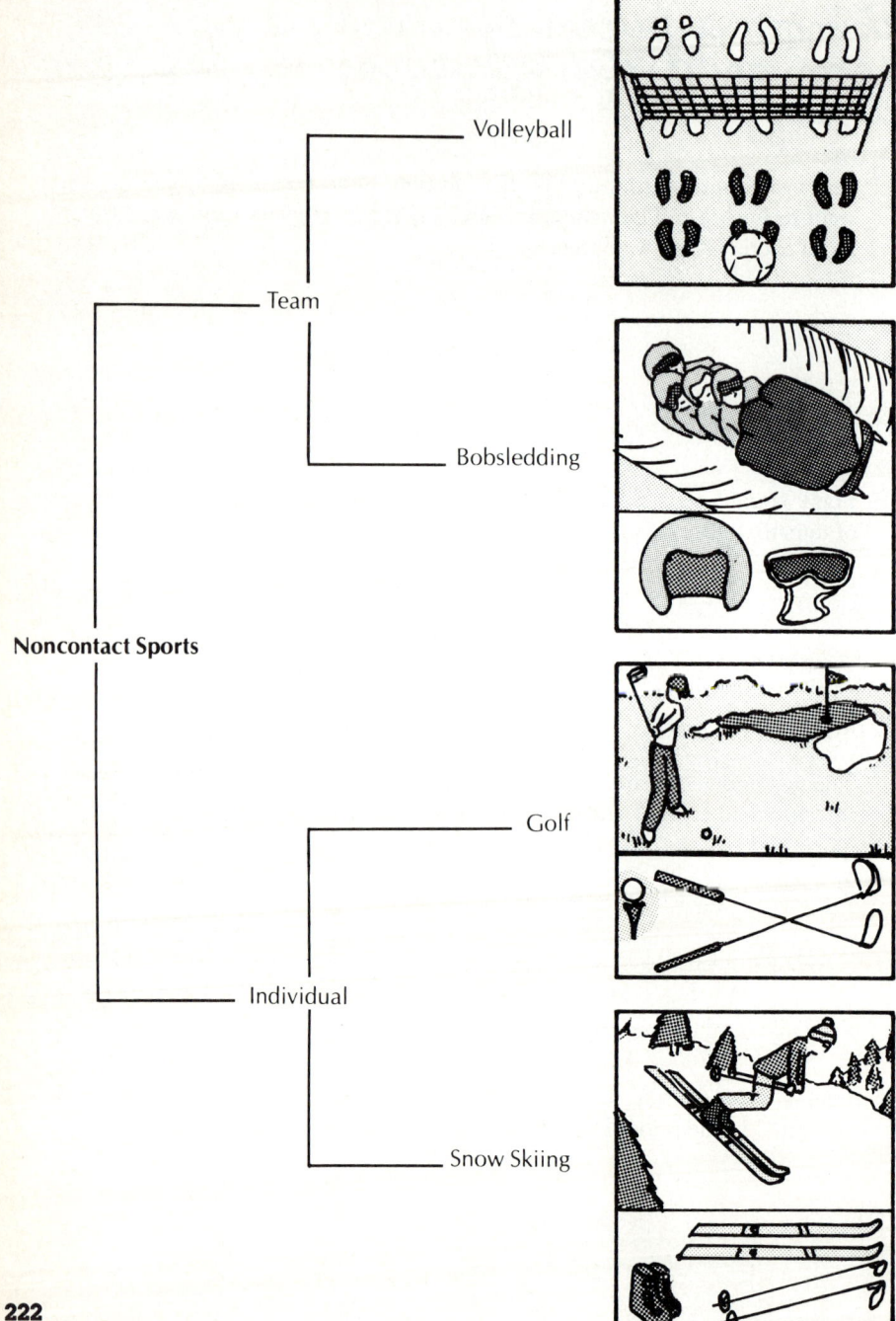

222

Imagine that a magazine has asked you to explain something about noncontact sports to an audience which knows little about sports. Use this classification chart and these pictures to guide you in writing an outline. Your outline should show that your composition will have two major paragraphs. Be sure to mark your major points and additional details clearly. Look back at the outline of Model Composition 14 if you need extra help.

Helpful vocabulary: players
volleyball court
volleyball
net
bobsledders
icy
chute/track
bobsled
goggles
golfer
golf course
golf clubs
golfball
tee
skis
poles
boots

Helpful phrases: A skier skis on . . .
A bobsledding team runs on . . .

Main idea sentence: _____

_____

_____

_____

_____

_____

Outline:

STUDENT COMPOSITION 14
Noncontact Sports

Stepping Along

Step 1: Use your outline to help you write a composition. In addition to your major paragraphs, write an introduction paragraph using your main idea sentence and a conclusion. Use appropriate transitions.

Step 2: Exchange your composition with a partner. As you read your partner's composition, think about these questions:
-Is everything in your partner's composition clear to you?
-Can you give your partner three suggestions for improvement?

Step 3: Talk with your partner about your compositions. Try to agree on improvements you can make.

Step 4: Rewrite your composition, making any changes you feel are necessary.

Further steps: As directed by your teacher.

MODEL COMPOSITION 15
The Uses of Cattle

Uses of Cattle
- Food
- Power
- Commercial Products
- Entertainment

Cattle are important animals in many parts of the world, and people use them in a variety of ways. These uses can be classified into four major categories: food, power, commercial products, and entertainment.

First of all, cattle are very important for the world's food supply. Over 50% of the meat we eat is beef or veal. Cattle also supply 95% of the world's milk.

In addition, cattle are an important source of power, especially in less-developed countries. They are used in agriculture to pull plows and carts in parts of central Europe, Africa, and Asia. In countries such as Senegal and Chad, cattle serve as pack animals.

The third major use of cattle is for various commercial products. For instance, glue is made from their bones, and leather goods such as bags and shoes are made from their hides. Cow hair is used in some blankets, carpets, and brushes.

Finally, cattle can provide us with entertainment. A savage breed of cattle is used for bullfighting in countries such as Spain, Mexico, and Venezuela. Cattle also play an important role in the rodeo, a popular spectator sport in the western half of the United States.

These, then, are the four major uses of cattle. We can see why these animals have such importance in many areas of the world.

ORGANIZATION

Outlining

Examine the following incomplete outline of the model composition. Can you complete it?

Outline of Model Composition 15

Introduction
I. Food
   A. Meat
      1. _____
      2. _____
   B. Milk
II. Power
   A. Agriculture
   B. _____
III. _____
   A. Glue (from bones)
   B. Leather goods (from hides)
   C. Blankets, carpets, brushes (from cow hair)

IV. _____
   A. _____
   B. _____

Conclusion

EXERCISE 15-A Classification Charts

Look at the following names.

    John Kennedy   George Washington
    General de Gaulle   Winston Churchill
    Queen Victoria   Victor Hugo
    Ernest Hemingway   Abraham Lincoln
    Charles Dickens   Virginia Woolf
    Mark Twain   Rousseau
    Louis XVI

There are several different ways in which these people can be classified. One way is to classify them according to the century in which they achieved worldwide fame. The classification chart would then look like this.

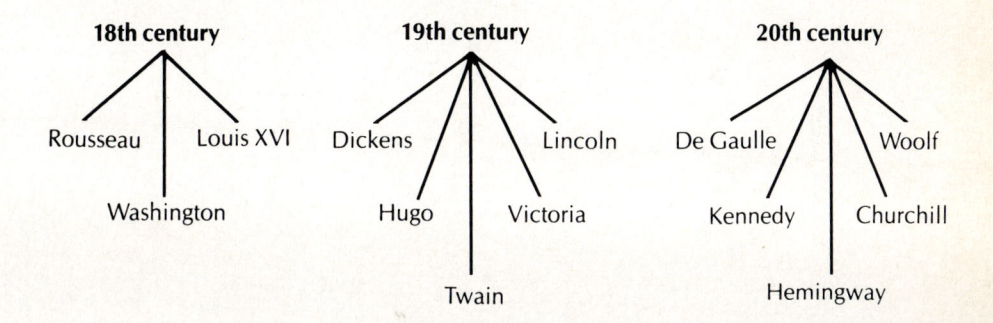

18th century
- Rousseau
- Louis XVI
- Washington

19th century
- Dickens
- Lincoln
- Hugo
- Victoria
- Twain

20th century
- De Gaulle
- Woolf
- Kennedy
- Churchill
- Hemingway

With the help of your classmates and your instructor, think of one or two other ways to classify the names and make the charts in the space below.

EXERCISE 15-B Main Idea Sentences and Introductions

Write an introduction for each of the following classification compositions. Remember that your main idea sentence should tell the reader *what* you are going to classify and *how* you will divide your subject.

1. _____

_____

_____

_____

_____

_____

   Land snails live in damp, shady places under logs and stones, at the edges of ponds and rivers, and in woods. In tropical forests, some even live in trees. Most land snails use lungs to breathe.
   Fresh-water snails live in rivers, ponds, lakes, and hot springs. Some kinds have lungs and must come to the surface of the water to breathe oxygen from the air. Others have gills, which take oxygen directly from the water.
   Salt-water or marine snails are the largest group of snails. Some types live along the seashore, and others live on the ocean floor. Most marine snails have gills.

2. _____

_____

_____

_____

_____

_____

Natural pearls are the most valuable kind of pearls. They are produced when a grain of sand or a tiny animal enters an oyster's shell. Gradually, the oyster completely covers it with layers of a substance called nacre.

Cultured pearls are real pearls that are made by oysters but with human help. A small mother-of-pearl bead is placed in the oyster's shell. The finished pearl has fewer but thicker layers of nacre than the natural pearl.

Imitation pearls are the last type of pearl and are made entirely by man. Manufacturers coat glass beads with pearl essence. This is a creamy liquid which is extracted from fish scales.

3. _____

_____

_____

_____

_____

_____

Some kinds of cloth are made from fibers obtained from animals. For example, wool comes from the fleece of certain kinds of sheep. It is a warm fabric and a natural insulator. Silk is made from fibers which are spun by silkworms. It is a light but warm fabric.

Other fabrics are made from plant fibers. Fibers from the cotton plant are spun into cotton cloth. The resulting fabric is light and comfortable. Linen also comes from plants. It is thicker than cotton and is made from the fibers of the flax plant.

Synthetics, fabrics that are not from animals or plants, are made by man. They are usually cheaper and easier to care for than natural fabrics. Orlon, for example, resembles wool but is easily washable. It is made from a chemical. Dacron, which resists fading and wrinkling, is made from coal, water, limestone, and natural gases.

EXERCISE 15-C Conclusions

Add a one-sentence conclusion to each of the short compositions in Exercise 15-B.

1. _____

_____

_____

CLASSIFYING 233

2.

3.

EXERCISE 15-D Transition Review

The following composition does not read smoothly because it contains no transitions in the major paragraphs. Rewrite it, using appropriate transitions.

      There are thousands of different diseases in the world, and new ones are discovered all the time. However, they can all be classified into two categories: infectious and noninfectious.
      Infectious diseases are caused by bacteria or viruses. They can be passed from person to person by close contact. The common cold and influenza are infectious diseases. Tuberculosis, a lung malady, is an infectious disease.

Noninfectious diseases are usually caused by bodily malfunction or a genetic problem. They cannot be transmitted from one person to another. Heart disease is a noninfectious disease which is becoming common for both men and women. A noninfectious disease is cystic fibrosis. It strikes young children and is usually fatal.

Scientists continue to discover new diseases. Any new disease, however, is still classified as either infectious or noninfectious.

Rewritten composition

CLASSIFYING 235

_____

_____

_____

_____

Giving Examples with *Such As*

You have learned that when you give examples you can use the transitions *for example, for instance, also,* and *another.* If you wish to list your examples as briefly as possible, you can use *such as* + your specific examples immediately following your general word or phrase.

EXAMPLE

Cattle also frequently serve as pack animals in countries *such as* Chad and Senegal.

Find additional examples in the model composition.

EXERCISE 15-E

Read the following groups of sentences. Then combine each group into one sentence using *such as.* Omit *some* in your new sentence.

1. Some parts of the world remain virtually unexplored. For instance, the Arctic and Antarctica have not been explored much. Neither have the Himalayas or the Amazon Basin.

   Parts of the world such as the Arctic, Antarctica, the Himalayas, and the Amazon Basin remain virtually unexplored.

2. Some birds cannot fly. For instance, penguins cannot fly. Neither can ostriches.

3. Some athletes are internationally known. The soccer player Pele and the boxer Muhammad Ali are both famous around the world.

4. Some countries have more than one official language. For example, Switzerland has more than one official language. So do Norway and Yugoslavia.

5. In the twentieth century, some presidents were elected to the White House more than once. Franklin Roosevelt was elected four times, for example. Richard Nixon and Woodrow Wilson were each elected twice.

6. There are a number of causes of insomnia. Stress is one common cause. Physical discomfort is another. Coffee-drinking before bedtime may also result in a lack of sleep.

GRAMMAR AND PUNCTUATION

EXERCISE 15-F Punctuation Review

Punctuate these sentences correctly.

1. Although Beethoven became totally deaf at age forty-six he continued writing great music.

2. The helicopter for instance is one type of motorized aircraft.

3. The United States Armed Forces are divided into four groups the Army the Navy the Air Force and the Marines.

4. She doesn't read English however she speaks it very well.

5. The world's oil supply is shrinking so oil is increasing in value.

6. After they went to New York City they visited Peoria Illinois.

7. Scientists are interested in the theory of black holes because it may explain the origin of the universe.

8. On April 4 1968 Martin Luther King, Jr. was fatally shot in Memphis Tennessee.

9. Jupiter the largest planet has a diameter of 88000 miles.

10. Bamboo is used for two purposes for food and for commercial products.

11. The Venus flytrap a plant which eats flies and other insects lives in coastal areas.

12. The five largest countries in the world are the Soviet Union Canada the People's Republic of China the United States and Brazil.

STUDENT OUTLINE AND COMPOSITION 15

Develop your own topic, or choose one of the topics below for your final classification composition. Consider your fellow students as your audience.

1. Choose an animal that is used for several different purposes and classify its uses. Horses, camels, elephants, llamas, and goats are just some of the animals which are used in a variety of ways. The major categories in your composition may be somewhat different from those in Model Composition 15. For example, you may need to include *transportation* as a category. When you give examples for each use of the animal, be as specific as possible. You can mention, for instance, *where* the animal is used for a specific purpose, *how widespread* the use is, or *why* the animal is used in a particular way. You may wish to look in the encyclopedia for more information about the animal you have chosen.
2. Explain the various holidays you celebrate in your country by classifying them.
3. Explain a topic in your major field by classifying it. For example, if your field is computer science, you might attempt to classify computers or computer software.
4. *CHALLENGER:* Think of all the methods you have used to improve your English or those you have heard of or would like to try. Explain these methods by classifying them.

Stepping Along

Step 1: After choosing your topic, "brainstorm" with other students who have chosen the same topic. You should write down any ideas that occur to you (in any order). For question 1, write down as many uses of the animal as you can think of. For question 2, write down names of holidays, and for question 4, various methods of learning English.

Step 2: Individually or in groups, organize your material by putting it in a classification chart or an outline. Think of a general heading for each of your groups.

Step 3: On your own, write a composition using your chart or outline. Remember to write an introduction and conclusion, and use appropriate transitions.

Step 4: Exchange compositions with someone you didn't work with on Steps 1 or 2. As you read your partner's composition, think about these questions:
-Is the introduction interesting?
-Are the general categories of the classification clear to you?
-Does your partner support each category with clear examples?

-Are transitions used appropriately?
-Can you give your partner any suggestions for improvement?

Step 5: Talk with your partner about the strong and weak points of your compositions.

Step 6: Rewrite your composition, making any changes you feel are necessary.

Further steps: As directed by your teacher.

UNIT SIX
Describing a Mechanism or a Process

INTRODUCTION

When you describe a mechanism or a process, you explain how something works or takes place by analyzing its parts or elements and then examining their relationship to each other. For example, you can explain how a barometer measures the pressure of the air by identifying its parts: a reservoir, mercury, a glass tube, and a scale, and then explaining how they function together. Or you can explain how the respiratory system works by analyzing what the diaphragm, nasal cavity, trachea, bronchial tubes, and lungs do so that we can breathe. There are several important things to remember when you explain a mechanism or a process.

1. *Be sure to include all major parts or elements.*
   Each major part or element has a particular function and contributes to make the mechanism or process work. Therefore, do not leave out any major part or element.
2. *Identify each part or element.*
   You can help your audience visualize each part or element by giving at least one of the following pieces of information: a description, the location, and/or the function. This applies mainly to mechanisms.
3. *Follow chronological order.*
   Chronological order is important when you explain how the parts or elements work together. For example, when describing how plants and animals become petrified, it is necessary to follow a certain order: 1) water dissolves away the original substance of the plant or animal, 2) minerals replace the dissolved substance. If you don't follow this order, the process of petrification will not be clear to the reader.

4. *Use accurate terminology.*
   You will often need to use technical terminology to name a part, a process, or a function. When this is necessary, do so. Don't, for instance, call one of the parts of a camera "a device that controls the amount of light that enters the lens." Call that device by its name, "shutter." You may find the right terminology in dictionaries, encyclopedias, or textbooks.
5. *Keep your audience in mind.*
   You must decide whom you are writing your composition for. For instance, your explanation of how a pacemaker works will be different depending on whether it is given to a medical student or to a general audience. In this unit, your writing will be geared to a very general audience. However, when you explain a mechanism or process to a specialized audience, the same principles apply.

People in different fields make use of this kind of organization when they write. A dental student, for instance, may need to describe the process of tooth decay, or a nuclear engineer may want to explain how a nuclear reactor works.

MODEL COMPOSITION 16
A Television

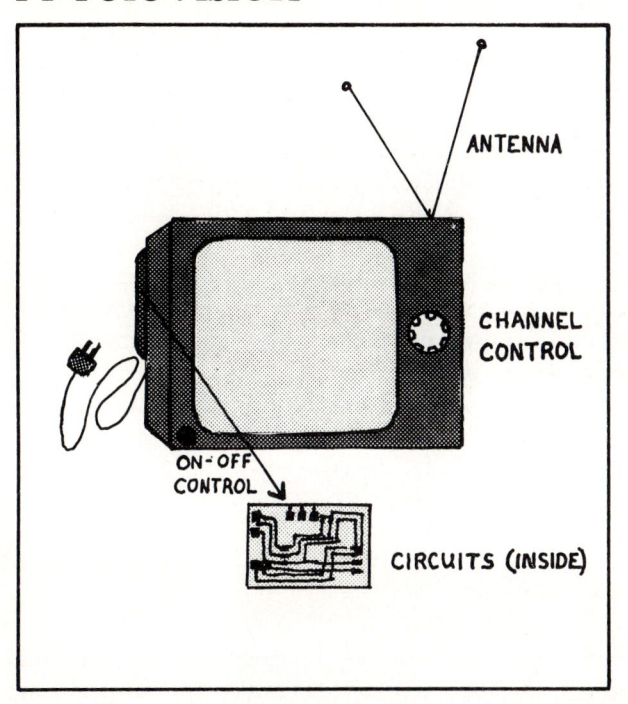

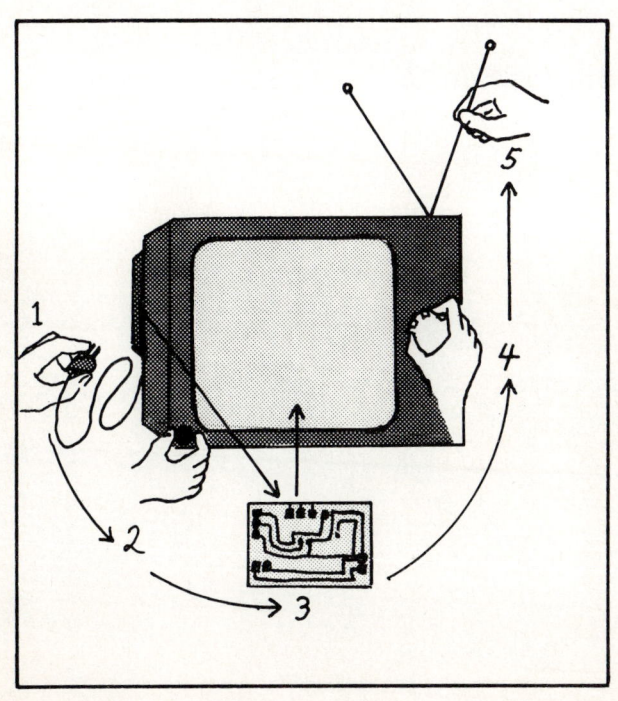

Televisions can be as large as a home movie screen or as small as a hand. They can be color or black-and-white. However, all televisions have the same basic parts: a body, circuits, a screen, various controls, an antenna, and a cord with a plug.

First, there is a box-shaped body. Inside the body are complex circuits, which amplify and separate the video and audio signals. Next is the screen made of glass, where the picture appears. There are also two major controls. One is the on-off control, which also alters the volume, and the other is the control which changes the channels. The antenna, a long, thin rod on the top of the set, improves the reception. Finally, there is the cord with a plug, which is plugged into a socket in the wall.

The parts work together as follows. First, the plug must be plugged into the socket, and the on-off control must be turned on. The circuits then send the picture to the screen. The channel control can be turned to choose a channel. If the picture is not clear, the antenna can be moved.

In summary, there are different types and sizes of televisions, but all have the same basic parts.

ORGANIZATION

Outlining

The following outline shows the organization of the model composition. Notice that the outline indicates two major paragraphs. The first paragraph identifies each part, and the second explains the operation of the parts.

Outline of Model Composition 16

Introduction

I. The parts
   A. Body
   B. Circuits
   C. Screen
   D. Controls
      1. On-off control
      2. Channel-changing control
   E. Antenna
   F. Cord with a plug

II. How the parts work together
   A. The plug must be plugged into a socket.
   B. The on-off control must be turned on.
   C. The circuits send the picture to the screen.
   D. The channel control can be turned to choose a channel.
   E. The antenna can be moved to make the picture clearer.

Conclusion

Main Idea Sentences and Introductions

When you describe a mechanism or a process, your main idea sentence should 1) name the mechanism or process, 2) either name the parts or elements or tell how many there are, and 3) possibly mention how or where the mechanism is used or when the process occurs.

EXAMPLES

Note how the following examples show the above points.

There are many kinds of watches,[1] but most have gears, a face, hands, a stem, and a watchband.[2]

The eye is a complex mechanism[1] which can be better understood when its eight major parts are analyzed.[2]

In order for plants to make food,[1] several elements must play a role: air, light, stomata, water, roots, and chloroplasts.[2]

The stapler,[1] a necessary tool in any office,[3] is composed of six major parts.[2]

EXERCISE 16-A

Read the following short compositions carefully. Each describes a mechanism. Choose the best main idea sentence for each.

1. First are the sharp cutting blades, which are made of steel. These cutting blades are joined in the middle by a small pivot pin, similar to a small screw. On top of the blades are round or oval handles, which provide openings for the thumb and first finger.

When the handles are pressed together with the thumb and first finger, the sharp blades meet and cut the material between the blades.

   a. Each pair of scissors has the same three basic parts.
   b. To use a pair of scissors, follow these simple steps.
   c. The mechanism I want to talk about has three basic parts.

2. The body of the electric beater is usually made of strong plastic and holds the motor. The handle, located on top of the body, makes the beater easy to hold. On the handle is the switch. It turns the motor on or off and controls the rotation speed of the beaters. The two oval-shaped beaters, which are made of strips of metal, are inserted into two holes in the underside of the body. Finally, there is the cord with a plug, which must be inserted into a wall socket.

   A beater works like this. When the cord is plugged into the wall, the switch can be turned on. The motor then begins to run. The motor activates the beaters, which begin to rotate. Now the beater is ready to beat the eggs.

   a. An electric beater makes cooking easy and works like this.
   b. An electric beater is composed of a body, a motor, a handle, a switch, two beaters, and a cord wtih a plug.
   c. An electric beater has three basic parts: the body, the handle, and the switch.

3. The frame of the bicycle is made of light metal and is triangular in shape. It is mounted on top of the two wheels. The pedals are square pieces, which are usually made of metal. These pedals are attached to a chain mechanism which drives the rear wheel. The handlebars, made for the hands to hold, are attached to the front wheel and control the steering. The seat, where the cyclist sits, is the triangular leather piece on the top of the frame.

   The parts work together in this way. The cyclist sits on the seat and pushes the pedals. The chain then begins to turn and drives the rear wheel. Once the bicycle is in motion, it can be steered by moving the handlebars right or left.

   a. Riding a bicycle, a popular form of recreation, is not difficult if you keep all of the bicycle parts in working order.
   b. All bicycles consist of these major parts: the frame, the wheels, the pedals, the chain, the seat, and the handlebars.
   c. The frame, the wheels, and the pedals are very important parts of the bicycle.

EXERCISE 16-B

Write an introduction for each of the three compositions in Exercise 16-A. Begin your introduction with a general statement. Then continue with the main idea sentence you have chosen.

1. _____
_____
_____
_____
_____
_____
_____
_____

2. _____
_____
_____
_____
_____
_____
_____
_____

3. _____
_____
_____
_____
_____
_____
_____
_____

Identifying the Parts of a Mechanism

When you describe a mechanism, it is necessary to name all the major parts. You should also **identify** each part. You can identify a part by giving one or more of the following pieces of information: 1) the *location* of the part, 2) a *description* of the part, or 3) the *function* of the part.

EXAMPLE

The following example from the model composition gives all three pieces of information about a television antenna.

The antenna, a long, thin rod *(description)* on the top of the set *(location)*, focuses the picture more clearly *(function)*.

EXERCISE 16-C

Look back at Model Composition 16. Tell which pieces of information *(location, description, function)* are given for each part.

EXERCISE 16-D

Look at the following pictures. Give the *location*, a *description*, and the *function* for each of the indicated parts. You will need the help of your dictionary or your teacher for some vocabulary items.

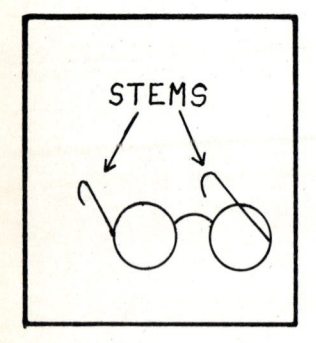

1. Location: *attached to the lenses*
   Description: *thin metal and/or plastic pieces*
   Function: *They hook on the ears and hold the glasses in place.*

DESCRIBING A MECHANISM OR A PROCESS **249**

[BUMPERS]

2. Location: _____

   _____

   Description: _____

   _____

   _____

   Function: _____

   _____

[SOFT DRINK CAP]

3. Location: _____

   _____

   Description: _____

   _____

   _____

   Function: _____

   _____

[WATCHBAND]

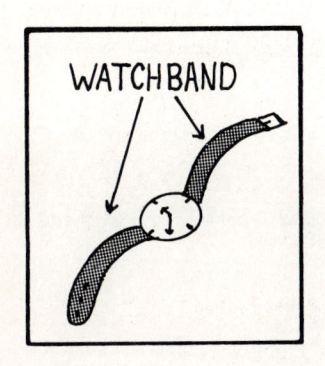

4. Location: _____

   _____

   Description: _____

   _____

   Function: _____

   _____

5. Location: _____

_____

Description: _____

_____

Function: _____

_____

GRAMMAR AND PUNCTUATION

Relative Clauses: Nonrestrictive

In this unit you will practice a grammatical structure which is very useful for describing mechanisms and processes. Look at the two sentences below.

The body contains complex ⌈circuits.⌉ ⌈These circuits⌉ amplify and separate the video and audio signals.

The second sentence repeats a noun from the first sentence. We can join the two sentences by dropping the second noun and substituting *which*. *Who* is used when referring to people. The part of the sentence which begins with *which* or *who* is called a **relative clause**. This clause must be placed immediately after the noun or noun phrase it modifies, as in the two examples below. Notice the punctuation.

The body contains complex circuits. ~~These circuits~~ *which* amplify and separate the video and audio signals.

The body contains complex circuits, *which amplify and separate the video and audio signals.*

Notice how the two sentences below can be joined by using a relative clause.

⌈The antenna⌉ improves the reception. ⌈The antenna⌉ is a long, thin rod on the top of the set.

The antenna ~~improves the reception. The antenna~~ *which* is a long, thin rod on the top of the set.

The antenna, *which is a long, thin rod on the top of the set,* improves the reception.

This type of relative clause is called a **nonrestrictive clause.** It adds extra but nonessential information about the noun or noun phrase it modifies. If we remove it from the sentence, the meaning of the sentence does not change in an important way. Nonrestrictive clauses are set off by commas in writing and slight pauses in speech.

EXERICSE 16-E

Make the second sentence in each pair a nonrestrictive relative clause, and insert it into the blank in the first sentence.

1. One major control is the on-off control, *which also alters the volume*.

   (The on-off control also alters the volume.)

2. An atomic nucleus, _____, contains protons, neutrons, and electrons.

   (An atomic nucleus is the central core of an atom.)

3. One part of the engine is the spark plugs, _____.

   (The spark plugs ignite the gasoline.)

4. The skin, _____, has three main layers.

   (It is the body's largest organ.)

5. Standard time is calculated from Greenwich, _____.

   (Greenwich is located in England.)

6. Arteries, _____,
   carry blood from the heart to the tissues.

   (Arteries are usually thick-walled and elastic.)

EXERCISE 16-F

Make the second sentence in each pair below a nonrestrictive relative clause. Then combine the sentences. Be sure to insert the relative clause in the right place.

1. Thin wires produce the heat in an electric blanket.
   The wires are sewn between two layers of material.

   Thin wires, which are sewn between two layers of material, produce the heat in an electric blanket.

2. Genes are units of heredity.
   Genes are found in chromosomes.

3. The layer above the troposphere is the stratosphere.
   The stratosphere extends to an altitude of about fifty kilometers.

4. The stomach can hold two to four liters of food.
   It is essentially a collapsible, elastic bag.

5. Meteors are small fragments of matter moving through the solar system.
   They frequently collide with the earth.

6. The speed of an electric sewing machine is usually regulated by a foot treadle.
   The foot treadle is located on the floor.

7. A supernova is sometimes visible in daylight.
   It is a star of spectacular brightness.

EXERCISE 16-G

Use each picture to form two sentences with nonrestrictive relative clauses. Your two sentences will emphasize different pieces of information.

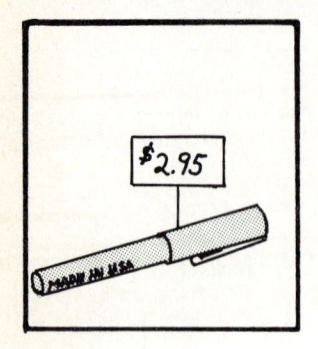

1. This pen, *which was made in the USA, costs $2.95.*

   This pen, *which costs $2.95, was made in the USA.*

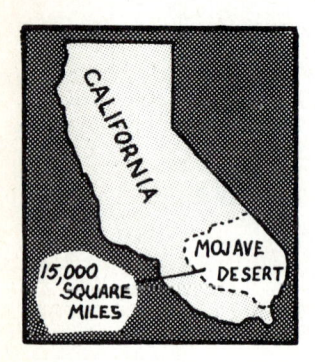

2. The Mojave Desert _____

   The Mojave Desert _____

DESCRIBING A MECHANISM OR A PROCESS   **255**

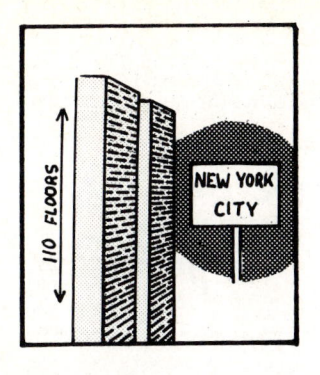

3. The World Trade Center Towers _____
   _____
   _____

   The World Trade Center Towers _____
   _____
   _____

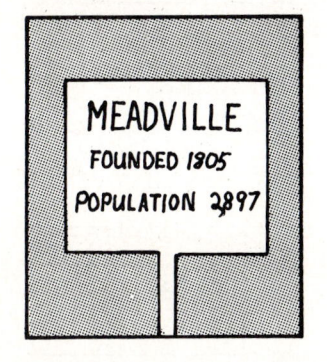

4. Meadville _____
   _____
   _____

   Meadville _____
   _____

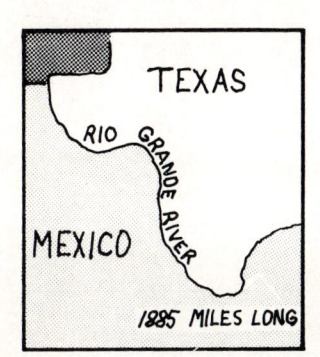

5. The Rio Grande River _____
   _____
   _____

   The Rio Grande River _____
   _____
   _____

EXERCISE 16-H

Look back at Exercise 16-D. Write sentences with relative clauses using at least two pieces of information about the parts.

1. The stems, which hook on the ears, are thin metal or plastic pieces.

2.

3.

4.

5.

STUDENT OUTLINE 16
An AM/FM Radio

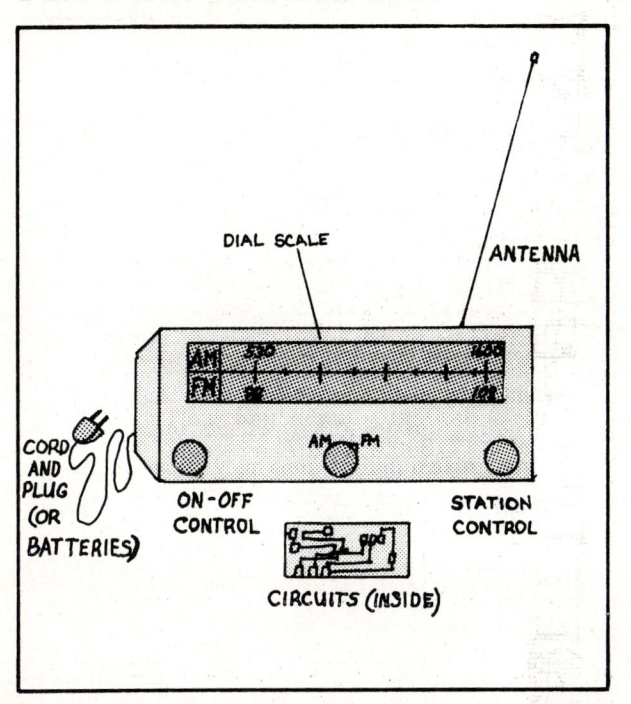

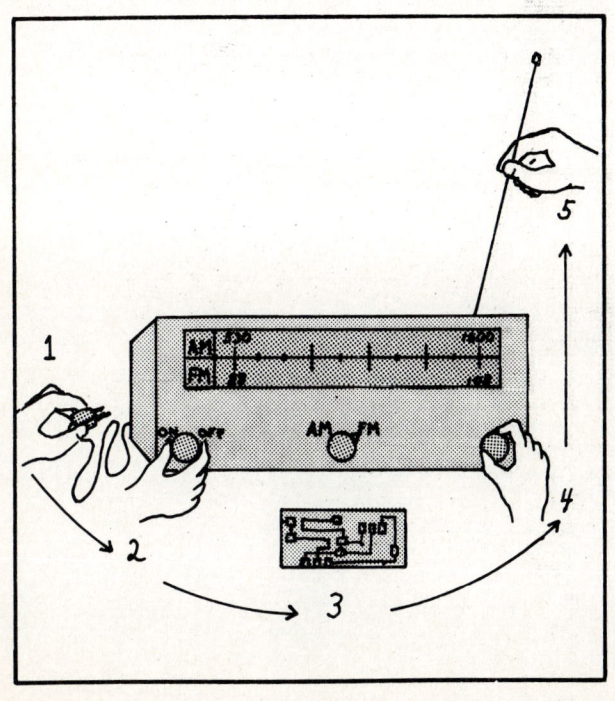

258 BASIC COMPOSITION FOR ESL

Imagine that you are employed as a writer for an electronics firm. They have asked you to explain how a radio works for a handbook for new trainees. These two pictures show you the major parts of an AM/FM radio and how the parts work together. Use the first picture for your main idea sentence and for the first major section of your outline (The parts). Use the second picture for the second major section (How the parts work together). If you need extra help, check the outline of Model Composition 16.

       Helpful vocabulary: rectangular or square (body)
                                        station
                                        sound
                                        battery-operated

Main idea sentence: _____

_____

_____

_____

_____

Outline:

STUDENT COMPOSITION 16
An AM/FM Radio

Stepping Along

Step 1: Use your outline to help you write a composition. In addition to your major paragraphs, write an introducton using your main idea sentence and a conclusion.

Step 2: Exchange your composition with a partner. As you read your partner's composition, think about these questions:
-Is everything in your partner's composition clear to you?
-Is paragraphing correct?
-Is each point sufficiently identified?
-Is each step mentioned in the correct order?
-Can you give your partner at least three suggestions for improvement?

Step 3: Talk with your partner about your compositions. Try to agree on improvements you can make.

Step 4: Rewrite your composition, making any changes you feel are necessary.

Further steps: As directed by your teacher.

MODEL COMPOSITION 17
The Human Respiratory System

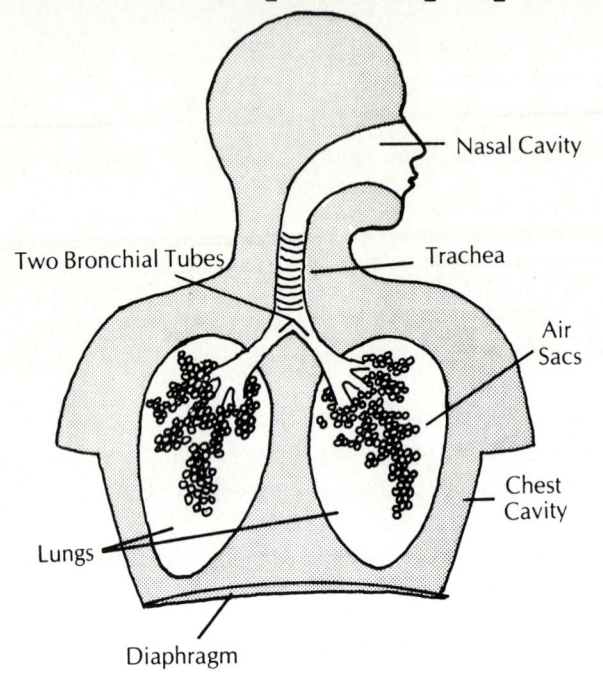

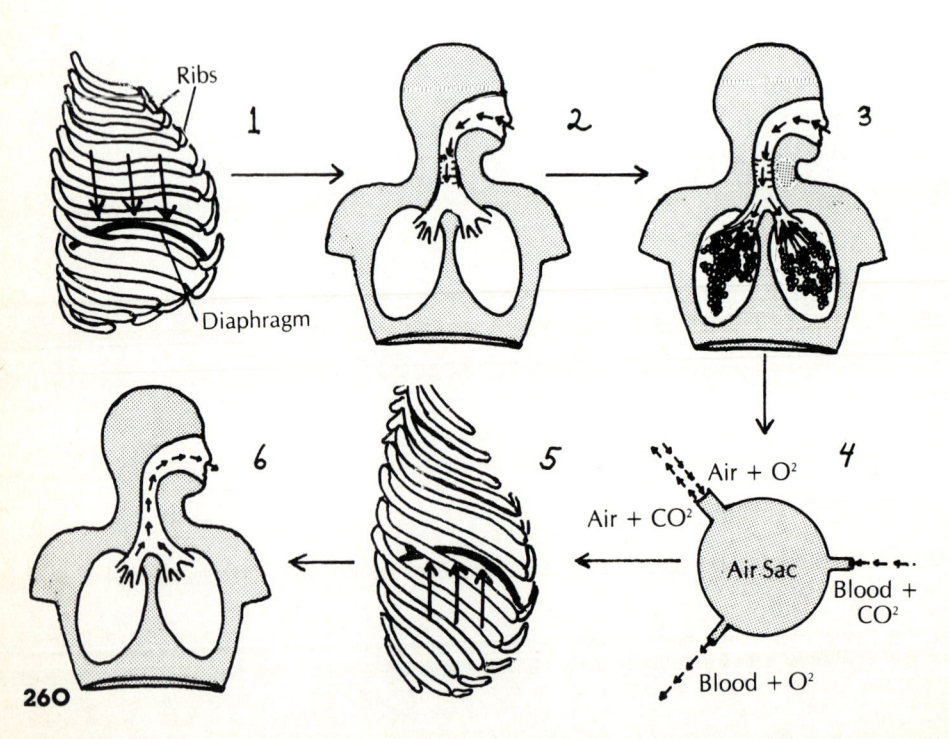

There are many mechanical systems, but none work better than the systems of the human body. One of these systems is the respiratory system. It consists of the lungs, the nasal cavity, the trachea, the bronchial tubes, and the diaphragm.

The lungs, which consist of millions of tiny air sacs, are located in the chest cavity. The nasal cavity, a system of membrane-lined passages, is in the head. The lungs are connected to the nasal cavity by a tube called the trachea. This tube separates into two bronchial tubes at its lower end. At the bottom of the chest cavity lies the diaphragm, a thick sheet of muscle that separates the chest cavity from the abdominal cavity.

This is how the respiratory system works. The diaphragm moves down, and the chest muscles lift the ribs. When this happens, air enters the nasal cavity through the nose. It passes into the trachea and moves to the lungs through the bronchial tubes. The air then flows into the air sacs, which are covered by blood vessels. These blood vessels take oxygen (O_2) from the air and release carbon dioxide (CO_2) back into the air sacs. The air that contains carbon dioxide is exhaled through the nose when the diaphragm moves up.

Each part of the respiratory system performs a particular function. We can breathe, then, because the parts work together so well.

ORGANIZATION

Outlining

Below is a partial outline of the model composition. Can you complete it?

Outline of Model Composition 17

Introduction
I. The parts
   A. Lungs
   B. Nasal cavity
   C. _____
   D. Bronchial tubes
   E. _____
II. How the parts work together
   A. The diaphragm moves down, and the chest muscles lift the ribs.
   B. _____
   C. Air passes into the trachea.
   D. The bronchial tubes take the air to the lungs.
      1. Air flows into the air sacs, which are covered by blood vessels.
      2. _____

E. The diaphragm moves up.
F. The air that contains CO_2 is exhaled through the nose.

Conclusion

Explaining the Operation of a Mechanism or Process

When you tell how a mechanism or process works, be sure to put the facts in chronological order. You will also want to use transitions which show this order. Can you list some? For additional help with transitions which show chronological order, look back at Unit One.

EXERCISE 17-A

Below are groups of sentences which describe how a mechanism or process works. Place the sentences of each group in proper order by numbering them. Then use the sentences to write a clear, logically ordered paragraph. You may use transitions, combine some of the sentences, change nouns to pronouns, and so on. Study the example.

1. Rain is formed in the following way.
   - **2** The water vapor is carried upward by the wind.
   - **3** The water vapor cools.
   - **1** Water evaporates.
   - **5** The water vapor condenses into drops and falls as rain.
   - **4** The rising-cooling process continues until the air can no longer hold the vapor.

Rain is formed in the following way. First, water evaporates. The water vapor is carried upward by the wind and then cools. The rising-cooling process continues until the air can no longer hold the vapor. Finally, the water vapor condenses into drops and falls as rain.

2. The digestive system works this way.
   - _____ The food passes from the stomach into the small intestine.
   - _____ The teeth chew the food.
   - _____ The stomach churns the food and adds digestive juice.
   - _____ The food passes through the esophagus and into the stomach.
   - _____ The food is swallowed.
   - _____ Pancreatic juice, intestinal juice, and bile complete the digestive process in the small intestine.

3. Coal is formed over a long period of time in the following way.

   _____ The plants begin to rot.

   _____ As the plant debris accumulates, peat is formed.

   _____ The pressure of the sediment slowly compacts the peat.

   _____ The peat is gradually transformed into coal.

   _____ The peat is covered by sediment.

   _____ Generations of plants grow and die in a humid environment.

EXERCISE 17-B Irrelevant Sentences

Read the following compositions. Find the sentence in each one which does not support the main idea sentence. Cross it out.

1.   Flashlights come in a range of sizes from pocket-sized miniatures to powerful hand-held searchlights. They all have the same basic parts: a body, a bulb, a socket, a reflector, a window, a spring, and a switch.
       First is the body, a hollow cylinder that contains the batteries. These provide the energy for most flashlights. At the top of the body is the bulb, which is inserted in a socket. This is usually attached to the reflector. The

reflector, which is made of aluminized plastic or metal, has a parabolic shape. Next is the window that covers the bulb. The spring is at the bottom end of the body and holds the batteries in place. Last is the on-off switch, usually placed on the body.

Here is how the parts work. First, the batteries must be placed inside the body. Next, the switch must be turned on. This causes the electrical current to move from the batteries to the light bulb. When the flashlight is on, the reflector concentrates the light in one direction. Flashlights can be purchased in any hardware store.

Big or small, then, all flashlights function in a similar manner.

2. In order for plants to make food, several elements must play a role: air, light, stomata, water, roots, and chloroplasts. The process, which takes place mostly in the leaves, is called photosynthesis.

First, plants need air. Air enters the plant through openings in the leaves called stomata. Stomata are located on the surface of leaves between cells. Another important element is light, which contains energy. Water is also necessary. It enters the plant through a network of underground tubes called roots. When you transplant a plant, be careful not to break these off. Last are the chloroplasts, which are oval green bodies located in the leaf cells and containing chlorophyll.

Photosynthesis works like this. Light is absorbed by the chloroplasts, and air enters the leaves through the stomata. At the same time, water is taken in by the roots and travels to the leaves. Energy from the light is used to split the water molecules into hydrogen and oxygen. The hydrogen molecules combine with carbon dioxide from the air and form a sugar-like compound. This is changed to carbohydrates which the plant uses for food.

In summary, plants need air, light, and water in addition to their own parts for the process of photosynthesis to take place.

3. Most of us take our ability to speak for granted. However, the production of voice is a complex process. The organs involved are the lungs, the trachea, the larynx, the vocal cords, the pharynx, the mouth, and the nose.

First there are the lungs, which provide the air necessary for voice production. Next is the trachea, a tube which connects the lungs to the larynx. The larynx is shaped like a box and contains the vocal cords. These are two bands of elastic tissue which are placed horizontally across the larynx and which can be pulled apart or closed. Finally, there is the pharynx, a tube which connects the larynx with the mouth and nose.

Voice is produced in the following way. When we exhale, air from the lungs travels through the trachea to the larynx. When the stream of air passes between the vocal cords, it causes them to vibrate. These vibrations are transmitted through the pharynx, and they emerge from the mouth or nose as voice. Men's voices are usually lower than women's.

In conclusion, our ability to speak depends on the proper functioning of all these parts.

GRAMMAR AND PUNCTUATION

EXERCISE 17-C Review: Nonrestrictive Relative Clauses

Fill in each blank with a nonrestrictive relative clause. The relative clause should give the information which is requested in the parentheses.

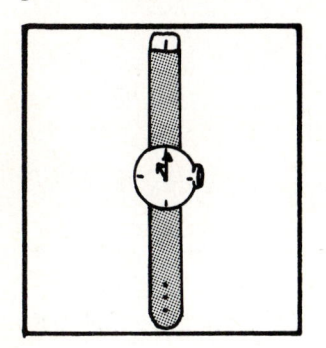

1. The stem of a watch, _____

   _____ , allows you to wind

   it. (location)

2. An eraser, _____

   _____ ,

   is made of rubber. (function)

3. The television screen, _____

   _____ ,

   is located on the front of the set. (description)

267

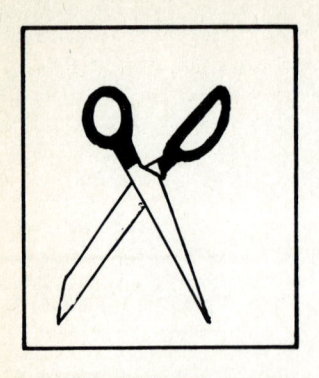

4. The handles of a pair of scissors, _____

_____,

make it easy for the thumb and first finger to hold. (description)

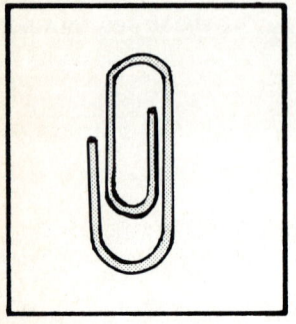

5. The paper clip, _____

_____,

is made of a single piece of twisted metal. (function)

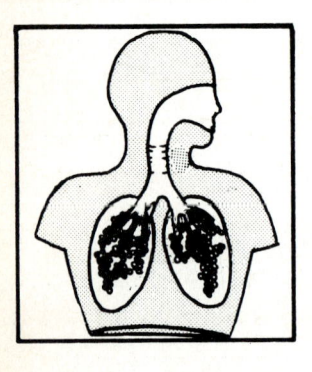

6. The air sacs, _____,

exchange CO_2 for O_2. (location)

Relative Clauses: Restrictive

Look at the two sentences below.

1. The lungs, which are located in the chest, consist of millions of tiny air sacs.

2. The trachea is a tube {that / which} connects the nasal cavity to the lungs.

In example 1, we can remove the relative clause, and the meaning of the sentence does not change in an important way. As you already know, this is called a nonrestrictive clause. Example 2 contains a **restrictive clause.** A restrictive clause gives essential information about a noun or noun phrase that sets it apart from the others in the same group. The restrictive clause in example 2 tells what makes the trachea different from other tubes in the body, such as the esophagus or the bronchial tubes. We cannot remove a restrictive clause from the sentence because it gives essential information about the noun or noun phrase it modifies. A restrictive clause is *never* set off by commas. When the noun preceding the restrictive clause refers to a thing, the relative clause is introduced with *that* or *which*.

EXERCISE 17-D

Make a restrictive clause from the second sentence in each pair below, and insert it into the blank in the first sentence. You may use either *that* or *which*.

1. The knob *which is on the right of the stove* controls the oven temperature.
   The knob is on the right of the stove.

2. The heart is a muscle _____ .
   The muscle pumps blood.

3. The control _____
   regulates the water level in the washing machine.
   The control is labeled ''Low,'' ''Medium,'' and ''High.''

4. The trachea is a tube _____ .
   The tube is made of rings of cartilage.

5. The tachometer is a gauge _____ .
   The gauge is marked in rpms.

6. The tube _____
   is called the Eustachian tube.
   The tube connects the middle ear to the throat.

EXERCISE 17-E

Make one sentence out of the following pairs. Make the second into a restrictive clause.

1. This is the machine.
   The machine grinds meat.

   This is the machine that grinds meat.

2. The reflector is a cup-shaped structure.
   This structure concentrates the beam of light.

   _____

   _____

3. The structure is named the cochlea.
   The structure receives vibrations from the middle ear.

   _____

   _____

4. The hormone is called secretin.
   The hormone causes the pancreas to secrete.

   _____

   _____

5. A tendon is a cord of tissue.
   The cord of tissue attaches a muscle to a bone.

   _____

   _____

6. The ductless gland is called the pituitary gland.
   The ductless gland secretes a growth hormone.

   _____

   _____

DESCRIBING A MECHANISM OR A PROCESS

EXERCISE 17-F

Attach a restrictive clause to the noun which is followed by a blank. You can use either *that* or *which*.

1. Evaporation is the process *that changes a liquid into a vapor*.

2. The roots are the part of the plant _____.

3. Animals _____ are called birds.

4. The face of a clock contains a set of hands _____.

5. Solar energy is energy _____.

6. The satellite _____ is the moon.

7. Soap and detergent are chemical agents _____.

Relative Clauses: Omitting the Relative Prounoun + the Form of *To Be*

In restrictive and nonrestrictive clauses, the relative pronoun *(which, that,* or *who)* + the form of **to be** *(is, are, was, were)* can usually be dropped.

EXAMPLES

The nasal cavity, *which is a system of membrane-lined passages,* is in the head.
The nasal cavity, *a system of membrane-lined passages,* is in the head.

The knob *which is on the right* controls the volume.
The knob *on the right* controls the volume.

EXERCISE 17-G

Look back at Model Composition 17. Underline once all examples of complete relative clauses. Underline twice all examples of relative clauses where the relative pronoun + *to be* has been omitted. Tell if each clause is restrictive or nonrestrictive.

EXERCISE 17-H

Cross out the relative pronouns + forms of *to be* wherever possible.

1. At the bottom of the chest cavity lies the diaphragm, ~~which is~~ a thick sheet of muscle.
2. The heart is a muscle which pumps blood.
3. The antenna, which is a long, thin rod on the top of the set, improves the reception.
4. The knob which is in the middle controls the oven temperature.
5. Silk, which was first discovered in China, is made from the cocoons of silkworms.
6. The antenna, which focuses the picture more clearly, is on top of the set.
7. The nasal cavity is connected to the lungs by a tube which is called the trachea.
8. X-rays, which are invaluable in science, medicine, and industry, are very short electromagnetic rays.
9. Gastric juices are juices in the stomach that digest food.
10. The button that is on the top will turn the computer on.

STUDENT OUTLINE 17
The Human Circulatory System

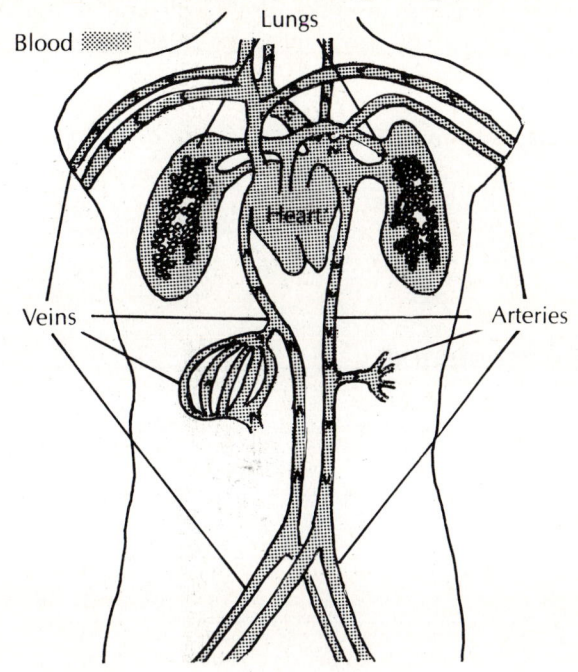

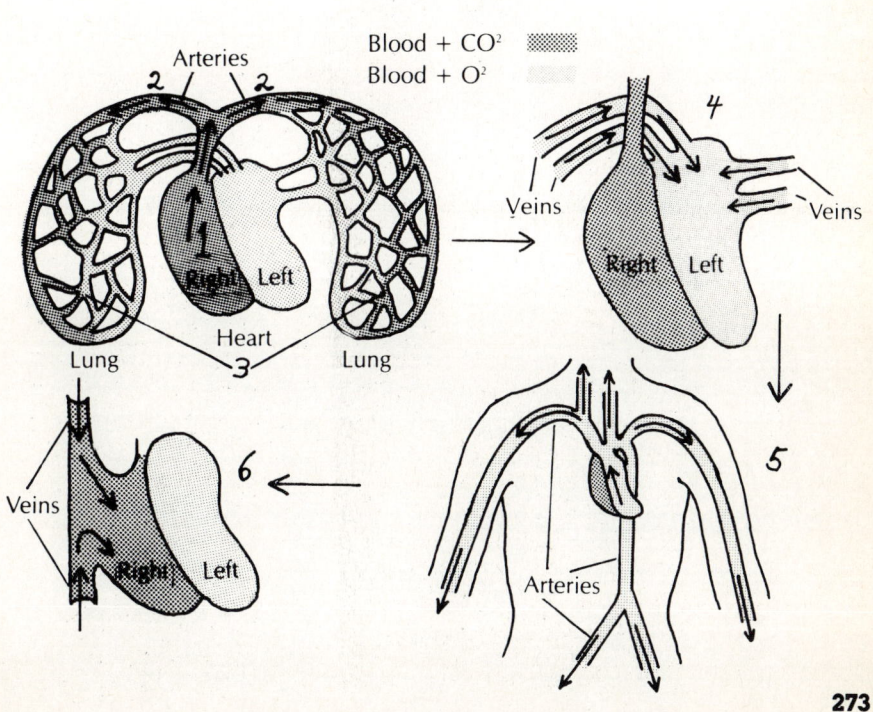

274　BASIC COMPOSITION FOR ESL

Suppose that you are working for a medical organization. Your boss has asked you to write a brief description of the human circulatory system for a brochure on CPR (cardiopulmonary resuscitation) for the general public. These pictures show you the main parts of the system and how that system works. Use the pictures as a guide, and write an outline and an introduction. You may want to use an encyclopedia or your dictionary for additional help.

Helpful vocabulary:　muscle
pump
contract
flow through the arteries and veins
drop CO_2
pick up O_2

Main idea sentence: _____

_____

_____

_____

_____

Outline:

STUDENT COMPOSITION 17
The Human Circulatory System

Stepping Along

Step 1: Use your outline to help you write a composition. In addition to your major paragraphs, write an introduction paragraph using your main idea sentence and a conclusion.

Step 2: Exchange your composition with a partner. As you read your partner's composition, think about these questions:
-Is everything in your partner's composition clear to you?
-Is paragraphing correct?
-Underline the relative clauses in your partner's composition. Is the punctuation correct? Do the main clause and the relative clause both have verbs?
-Can you give your partner at least three suggestions for improvement?

Step 3: Talk with your partner about your compositions. Try to agree on improvements you can make.

Step 4: Rewrite your composition, making any changes you feel are necessary.

Further steps: As directed by your teacher.

MODEL COMPOSITION 18
Earthquakes

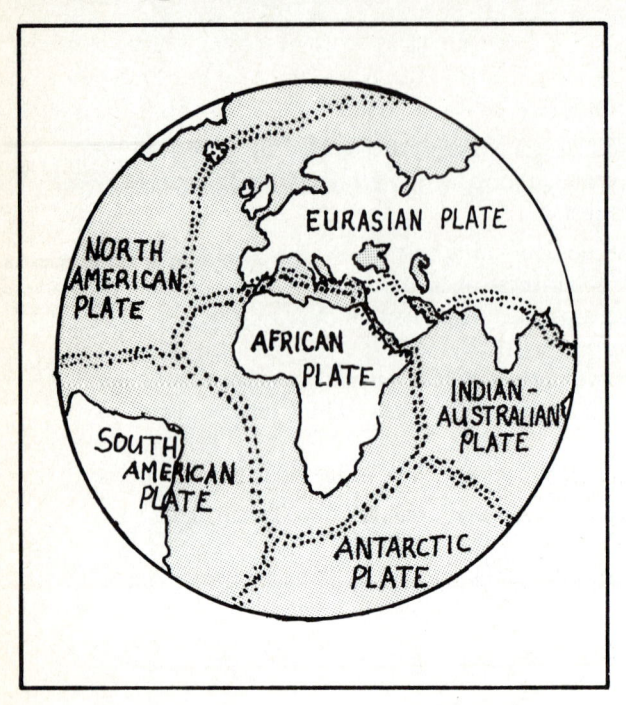

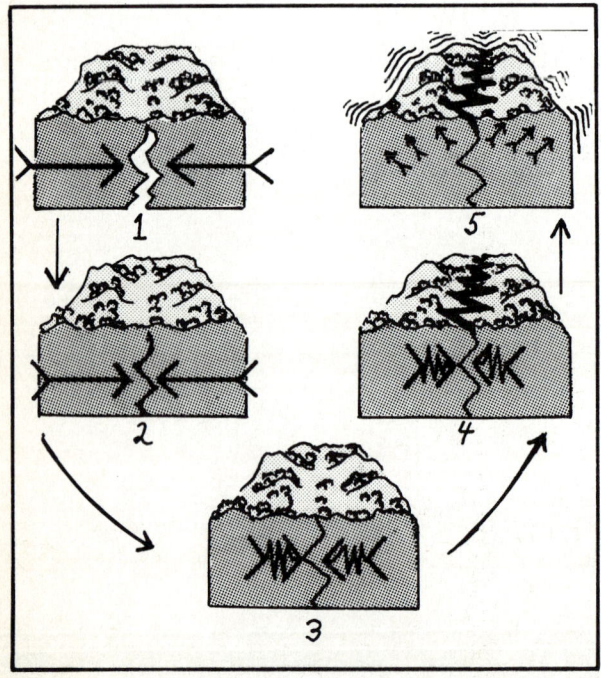

Earthquakes occur all over the world. Although we cannot predict them accurately or control their effects, we understand how earthquakes happen. According to modern scientists, earthquakes can be explained by mobile, platelike segments which cover the surface of the earth.

There are a dozen or more of these large, restless plates, which are each about seventy miles thick. They move slightly each year due to unknown forces deep within the earth. The places where these plates meet are called fault lines. These fault lines are generally earthquake areas.

An earthquake is produced in the following way. First, two or more plates bump against each other with great force. If the plates lock together, as they often do, pressure builds up. When the pressure becomes very strong, the earth cracks. The energy is then released in a burst of shocks, which can often be felt for great distances.

Scientists continue to study these natural disasters. One day, they hope to predict earthquakes before they happen and limit their effect on people and buildings.

ORGANIZATION

Outlining

Below is a partial outline of the model composition. Can you complete it?

Outline of Model Composition 18

Introduction

I. The components
   A. Large, restless plates
   B. _____

II. How an earthquake occurs

   A. _____
   B. The plates lock together.
   C. Pressure builds up and becomes strong.

   D. _____
   E. The energy is released in a burst of shocks.

Conclusion

DESCRIBING A MECHANISM OR A PROCESS   **279**

EXERCISE 18-A Introductions

Read the following compositions carefully and write an introduction for each one.

1. _____

_____

_____

_____

_____

_____

    The two rows of teeth consist of a large number of metal or plastic pieces that have small protrusions on the top and recesses on the underside. These teeth are held by the two strips of fabric tape. There is also the metal or plastic slide, which can be moved back and forth to open or close the zipper. The small end pieces are located at the ends of the rows of teeth to prevent the slide from coming off.
    The zipper works like this. When the slide is pulled in one direction, it draws the two rows together and interlocks the teeth. When the slide is moved in the opposite direction, the teeth separate, and the rows draw apart.

2. _____

_____

_____

_____

_____

_____

    The most important element is cream, which is extracted from milk. A high-quality cream will produce a good butter. Other important elements are the various pieces of equipment in the creamery. Large vats equipped with thermostats are used to pasteurize the cream.

280 BASIC COMPOSITION FOR ESL

    Mechanical, cylindrical drums equipped with paddles called baffles are used to churn the cream. Large wooden molds allow the butter to harden.
    Butter is made in this way. First, the creameries pasteurize the cream by heating and cooling it in the vats. When the cream reaches just the right temperature, it is put into the drums where the baffles churn it. This churning causes globules of fat from the cream to cluster together in masses called butter granules. The buttermilk is then drawn off, and the butter is washed with water and salted. Next, it is packed into the molds, where it hardens. Finally, the butter is cut into bricks, wrapped, and shipped to supermarkets.

3. _____

   _____

   _____

   _____

   _____

   _____

    The first element is the seed coat, an outer skin which protects the seed. Inside the seed is the embryo. It contains all the parts necessary for the growth of the plant. Another important element is the endosperm. This consists of one, two, or many seed leaves which nourish the embryo. Moisture is necessary too. One of its functions is to help dissolve certain food materials in the seed, so that these materials can be used for growth. The right temperature is also important for germination. Different seeds need different temperatures, and if the temperature is too high or too low, germination will not occur. The last important element is oxygen. Without it, the chemical changes which accompany growth cannot take place.
    A seed germinates in this manner. Moisture softens the seed coat and swells the tissues of the embryo. When the seed coat splits open, the embryo begins to grow. The root part starts growing downward. In many plants, the seed leaves separate and start to rise from the ground. In others, the seed leaves remain in the soil. Finally, the seed leaves dry up, and a pair of true leaves takes their place.

EXERCISE 18-B Conclusions

Write a one-sentence conclusion for each short composition in Exercise 18-A.

1. _____

2. _____

3. _____

GRAMMAR AND PUNCTUATION

EXERCISE 18-C Review: Relative Clauses

Label the second sentence in each pair as either "R" for restrictive clause, or "NR" for nonrestrictive clause. Punctuate where appropriate.

1. A rain gauge is used to measure the amount of rain that falls in a certain place or region during a certain period of time.

    NR This instrument, which is very simple, consists of a cylinder, a tube, a funnel, and a cover.

2. There are many different kinds of rocks.

   _____ Rocks which were created from molten lava are called volcanic rocks.

3. Picasso painted a great variety of pictures.

   _____ *Guernica* which depicts an incident in the Spanish Civil War is one of the most famous.

4. Different processes can be used to make synthetic natural gas.

   _____ Coal gasification for instance is a process which converts coal into synthetic natural gas.

5. One of the parts of a camera is the box.

   _____ This part which is completely dark inside holds the film.

6. Another part of the camera is the shutter.

   _____ This is the part which controls the amount of light reaching the film.

7. Mother Teresa of Calcutta won the 1979 Nobel Peace Prize.

   _____ The prize which consisted of $193,000 was awarded to her for her work in the slums of Calcutta.

8. The four principal temperature scales are the Fahrenheit, Celsius, Kelvin, and Rankine scales.

   _____ The scales which are the most widely used are the Celsius and the Kelvin.

9. A cell is composed of several different parts.

   _____ The part that surrounds the cell is called the cell membrane.

10. The Aesop fables date from the sixth century B.C.

    _____ These fables which are known all over the world were written by a Greek fabulist.

EXERCISE 18-D

Following are illustrations and statements which describe, first, the parts of a *flashlight* and, second, the parts which play a role in *voice production.* Practice combining various sentences using relative clauses. Write at least four sentences for each exercise.

1.

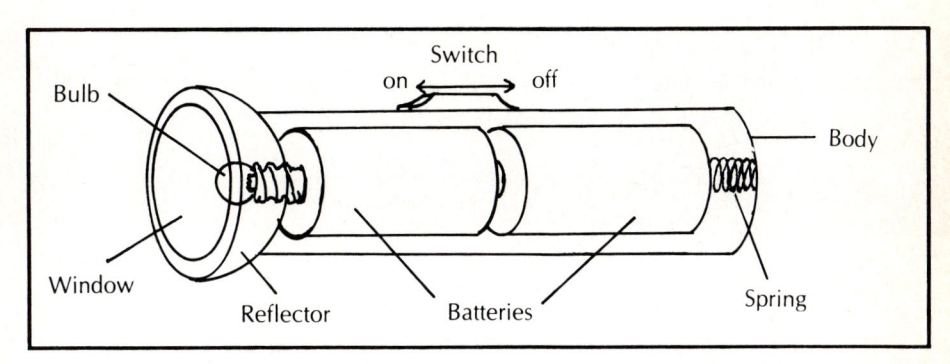

[Diagram of a flashlight with labeled parts: Bulb, Window, Switch (on/off), Body, Reflector, Batteries, Spring]

The body is a hollow cylinder.
The body contains the batteries.
The batteries provide the energy for the flashlight.
The bulb is attached to the reflector.
The reflector has a parabolic shape.
The reflector is made of aluminized plastic or metal.
The spring is at the bottom end of the body.
The spring holds the battery in place.

a. _____

b. _____

c. _____

d. _____

2.

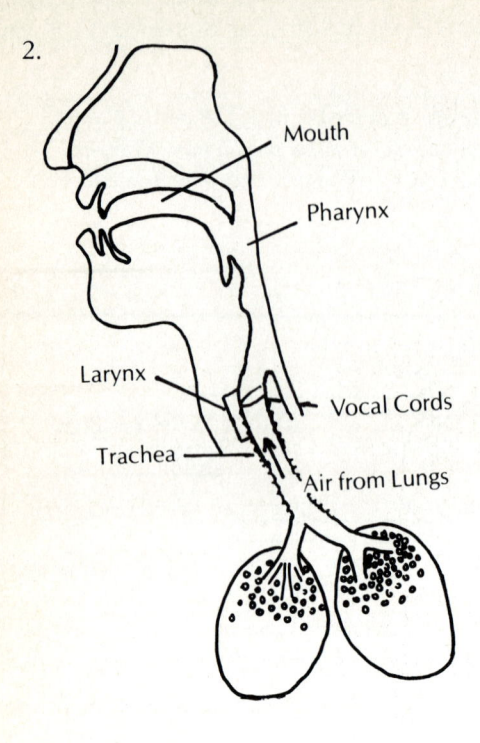

The lungs consist of millions of tiny air sacs.
The lungs provide the necessary air for voice production.
The trachea is a cartilaginous tube.
The trachea connects the lungs to the larynx.
The larynx contains the vocal cords.
The vocal cords lie horizontally across the larynx.
The pharynx is a muscular tube.
The pharynx connects the larynx with the mouth and the nose.

a. _____

_____ .

b. _____

_____ .

c. _____

_____ .

d. _____

_____ .

STUDENT OUTLINE AND COMPOSITION 18

Develop your own topic, or choose one of the topics below for your final composition. Consider your fellow students as your audience.

1. Describe a simple, small mechanism with which you are familiar, and tell how it works. Have it in front of you as you write.

    Suggestions: *Cigarette lighter* (main parts: case, lighter fluid, wick, flint, flint wheel)
    Ballpoint pen (main parts: body, cap, push button, spring, ink cartridge)
    A blender (main parts: base, motor, blades, glass container, cover, cord with a plug, and controls)

2. Describe a part of the body, and explain how it functions. Consult an encyclopedia for help.

    Suggestions: *The eye*
    The ear

3. Choose a natural phenomenon. Describe briefly its essential components or elements, and then tell how it occurs. Consult an encyclopedia for help.

    Suggestions: *How hail forms*
    How stalactites form
    How a geyser erupts
    How a volcano erupts

4. *CHALLENGER:* Describe a mechanism which interests you or which relates to your main field of study, and tell how it works. Consult sources (books or knowledgeable people) for extra help.

    Suggestions: *How a solar energy furnace works*
    How a home computer works
    How a printing press works
    How a space ship takes off

Stepping Along

Step 1: After choosing your topic, take time to think, do research, and write an outline of your major points.

Step 2: Write a composition using your outline. Remember to write an introduction and a conclusion.

Step 3: Get into groups of three students. Read each other's compositions. As you read your partner's composition, think about these questions:
-Is the description complete or has the writer left out a part or a step?
-Is there anything in the composition that is not completely clear to you?
-Can you give the writer three suggestions for improvement?

Step 4: Talk with your partners about these questions and try to agree on improvements each of you can make.

Step 5: Rewrite your composition, making any changes you feel are necessary.

Further steps: As directed by your teacher.

GLOSSARY

Active sentence	a sentence in which the agent (the one who performs the action) is in subject position
	The police want that criminal.
	(The subject, *police,* performs the action.)
Additional details	sentences or parts of sentences which give examples to explain major points
Adverbial	a word or phrase which tells *when, where, how,* or *how often*
	She wrote a letter **this morning.**
	When you pass the light, go **left.**
	He yelled **loudly.**
	They **frequently** *call.*
Agent	a person or thing that performs an action
Appositive	a noun or a noun phrase that immediately follows another noun and that explains or defines the noun it follows
	William Shakespeare, **the famous English dramatist and poet,** *was born in 1564.*
Audience	person or people who will read what you write
Cause	something which produces a result or effect
Chronological order	an arrangement of events in the order in which they happen in time
Classification chart	a treelike diagram which helps you organize your ideas when classifying

Classifying	organizing ideas or items with similar characteristics into categories
Clause	a group of words which contains a subject and a verb
Colon	a punctuation mark (:) which is often used before a list or a series of items
	I met several people: Mr. Burke, Ms. Findley, Dr. Malone, and her daughter.
Comparative degree	the form of the adjective that is used when a person, thing, or group is compared to another person, thing, or group
	I am **taller** *than he is.*
	This car is **more expensive** *than those.*
Comparing	thinking or writing about the similarities between two things or people
Composition	a piece of writing about one central topic
Conclusion	the final portion of a composition which sums up the major points or makes a judgment based on these major points
Contrasting	thinking or writing about the differences between two things or people
Dependent clause	a clause which is used as part of a longer sentence, and which, because it is not grammatically complete, must be connected to a main clause to make sense
	The car will run **after the battery is replaced.**
	Because the car is not running, *I will take the bus.*
Direct speech	the exact words used by a speaker; in writing, direct speech is enclosed by quotation marks
	The instructor said, "The research paper is due tomorrow."
Effect	a result; something which is brought about by a cause or causes
General	not detailed; not precise
	The word "animal" is more general than the word "dog."
Identify	define; characterize; you can identify a part of a mechanism by giving its function, its location, or a description of it

Imperative	a form of the verb used to give instructions, make requests, and give orders, and formed with the base form of the verb without a pronoun
	Write *clearly.*
	Please **come** *here.*
Indirect object	the receiver of a direct object
	Marsha gave **John** *the book.*
	Give these copies to **Ms. Graves.**
Indirect speech	a restatement of the words used by a speaker
	The instructor said that the research paper was due the following day.
Introduction	the beginning portion of a composition which introduces the subject generally; an introduction includes a main idea sentence
Introductory phrase	a phrase which is placed at the front of the sentence
	At the age of sixty-nine, *Ronald Reagan became president of the United States.*
Irrelevant	not connected or not appropriate (An *irrelevant sentence* is a sentence in a composition which is not connected or related to the main idea sentence.)
Main clause	a clause which is used as part of a longer sentence, but which is grammatically complete and could be a separate sentence
	The car will run *after the battery is replaced.*
	Because the car is not running, **I will take the bus.**
Main idea sentence	a general statement which gives the central idea of a paragraph or a short composition and which is most often placed at the beginning of a piece of writing
Major points	those sentences in a composition which directly explain or support the main idea sentence
Nonrestrictive clause	a relative clause which adds extra but nonessential information about the noun or noun phrase it modifies; a nonrestrictive clause is *always* set off by commas
	The dog, **which behaves badly,** *should go to obedience school.*
	(The relative clause gives extra information about one dog.)

Noun phrase	a group of words which functions as a noun *Lime Street* *the hot yellow sand*
Objective report	an organized presentation of facts which tells about something that happened
Outline	a brief and general plan used to help writers organize their thoughts and ideas before writing
Paragraph	a group of related sentences which communicates one central idea
Parallel	similar; corresponding
Passive sentence	a sentence in which the subject receives the action *That criminal is wanted by the police.* (The subject, *criminal,* is the receiver of the action.)
Past continuous tense	used to refer to an action a) that was taking place when another action occurred *I* **was working** *on my paper when you called.* b) that was taking place at the same time as another action *Abe* **was cooking** *while I* **was gardening.**
Past tense	used to refer to something in the past *World War II* **ended** *in 1945.* *They* **were** *very happy.*
Phrase	a grammatical unit of two or more words without a verb
Preposition	a word which shows the relation between words *Please go* **with** *Leslie.* *Please go* **for** *Leslie.* *Please go* **to** *Leslie.*
Present continuous tense	used for: a) something that is happening now *We* **are studying** *biology this summer.* b) something that will happen in the future *Michael* **is traveling** *to Rome next year.*

Present tense	commonly used for: a) a general act or state in the present *They* **play** *tennis well.* *He* **lives** *near the university.* b) a habitual action or general truth *I* **study** *English every day.* *Water* **freezes** *at 0° Centigrade.*
Pronoun	a word that stands in place of a noun *He* **saw** *her at the opera.* (rather than *Paul* saw *Olivia* at the opera.)
Receiver	a person or thing that receives an action
Relative clause	a clause which modifies and is attached to a noun or a noun phrase
Restrictive clause	a relative clause which gives essential information about a noun or noun phrase that sets it apart from others in the same group; a restrictive clause is *never* set off by commas *The dog* **which behaves badly** *should go to obedience school.* (The relative clause sets one dog apart from others. It tells us which of the dogs should go to obedience school.)
Specific	detailed; precise *The word "dog" is more specific than the word "animal."*
Synonyms	two words that have the same or nearly the same meanings *big/large, unhappy/sad*
Transition	a word or phrase which is used to connect two ideas *Go straight for two blocks.* **Then** *turn right.* *She enjoyed the movie. Her husband,* **on the other hand,** *did not.*
Topic outline	an outline in which the major points are represented by nouns or noun phrases (topics) rather than complete sentences

INDEX

Active sentences, 218–20
Adjectives, comparative degree, 149, 186–89
Adverbials, 110–11
    with *go,* 36
After
    to introduce adverbial clauses, 110–11
    to show chronological order, 32
    to give instructions, 11–12, 24–25
After that, to show chronological order, 32–34
Although, to show contrast, 189–91
Analyzing by cause and effect. *See* Cause and effect
And, 23–24
    to join two independent clauses, 23
Another, for adding examples, 206
Appositives
    defined, 52
    punctuation with, 52–53
As . . . as, for comparison, 185
Audience
    considering, when writing, 1, 46
    describing for a specific, 242

Because, to show cause-effect, 107–10
Because of, to show cause-effect, 122–24
Before, 24–25, 110–11
    to show chronological order, 32
    in giving instructions, 11–12
Both, 169
    to show similarities, 144–45
    But, to show differences, 136–37, 145–47, 164–66

Capitalization, 80–82
Cause-effect relationship, 105–7
    understanding, 89–91
Cause and effect writing, 85–129
Chronological order
    in describing, 241, 263–65
    in giving instructions, 1
    in objective reporting, 43, 46–47
    transitions for, 4–5, 22
Classification charts, 197, 199–200, 229
Classifying, 195–240
Clauses
    adverbial, 110–11
    defined, 11
    dependent, 11
    independent, 23
    main, 11
    nonrestrictive, 250–56, 267, 281–82
    relative, 250–56, 267, 268–72, 281–84
    restrictive, 268–71, 281–82
Colons, 220–21
    to introduce series, 208
Commas
    with adverbial clauses, 110–11
    with appositives, 52–53
    with dates, 65
    with dependent clauses, 11–13
    with independent clauses, 23
    with introductory phrases, 50–51
    with numerals, 66
    with place names, 66
    in series, 13–14, 221
Comparative degree, 149

Comparatives, 186–89
Comparing and contrasting, 131–94
Comparing, explained, 131
Compositions, model. *See* Model compositions
Conclusions, 232, 281
    introductory phrases for, 184
Contrasting, explained, 131

Dates, commas in, 65
Dependent clauses, 11, 189
Describing, 241–287
Details, adding, 77–78, 91, 104–5, 119–20
Differences, 160
    finding, 139–43
Direct speech, 53

Effect. *See* Cause and effect writing
Examples, transitions for giving, 206–7
Explaining. *See* Describing

For example, used to introduce examples, 206
For instance, used to introduce examples, 206

General words, 196, 202–3
Go, using, to show directions, 36
Grammar and punctuation, 6–14, 23, 65–66, 80–82
    in cause-effect writing, 107–11, 122–27
    in comparison and contrast writing, 149–52
    with introductory phrases, 50
    for passive sentences, 218–20
    to introduce series, 13, 208–9
    for transitions, 162–65

However, to show contrast, 136–37, 162–63, 164–66

Identifying
    by description, 248–50
    by function, 248–50
    by location of parts in a mechanism, 248–50
Imperative, using for instructions, 26
Imperative clauses, combining, 11–12
Imperative verbs, 6
In conclusion, 184
In contrast, for transitions, 178

Indirect speech, 53, 54
    tense in, 53
    verbs for, 54, 67–69
Instructions, giving, 1–41
In summary, to begin conclusions, 184
Introductions, 135, 137–39, 203–5
    for classification writing, 206, 231
    for comparison and contrast writing, 181–83
    for describing, 246, 279–80
Introductory phrase
    defined, 50
    punctuation with, 50–52
Irrelevant sentences, 22–23, 162, 217–18, 265–66
    in cause-effect writing, 107
    defined, 22
    in objective reporting, 64–65

Likewise, to show similarity, 178
Lists, colon with, 208

Main clauses, 11
Main idea sentences, 3–4, 34–35, 78–80, 103, 203–5
    for comparing and contrasting, 181
    defined, 22
    to show differences, 173
    useful phrases for, 181
    to show similarities, 173
Main idea sentences, examples
    for cause-effect writing, 91, 92–94, 104–5, 118
    for comparing and contrasting, 136
    for describing, 245
    for giving directions, 32
    for giving instructions, 3–4, 15, 18, 21, 26
    for reports, 47, 57, 63
Major points, in cause-effect writing, 91, 104–5, 119–20
Model compositions
    cause-effect, 87–88, 102–3, 117–18
    classifying, 197–98, 214–15, 227–28
    comparing and contrasting, 133–34
    describing, 243–44, 261–62, 277–78
    giving directions, 31–32
    writing instructions, 2–3, 20–21
    objective reporting, 45–46, 62–63, 75–76
    showing similarities and differences, 159–60, 176–77

Neither, to show similarity, 166–70
Next, to show chronological order, 32
Nonrestrictive clauses, 250–56, 267, 281–82
Noun phrase, defined, 122–24
Numerals, commas with, 66

Objective, being, defined, 44
Objective reporting, 43–83
On the other hand, to show contrast, 147–49
Organization
    by outlines, 2–3, 21, 31–32
    point-by-point sequence, 177–78
Outlines, 2–3
Outlines, examples
    for cause-effect writing, 88, 103, 118
    for classifying, 198–99, 215–17, 228–29
    for comparing and contrasting, 132, 134–35, 161
    for describing, 244–45, 262, 278
    for giving instructions, 15, 21, 26–28
    for objective reporting, 46, 76–77
    to show point-by-point sequence, 177–78
Paragraphs, main idea sentences in, 4
Passive sentences, 218–20
Past continuous tense, 67–69
Past tense, for indirect speech, 53, 67–69
Phrase, defined, 50
Point-by-point arrangement, 132
Point-by-point sequence, 177–78
Precise, being, 43, 48–50, 63–64
    defined, 43
Prepositions with *go,* 36
Present continuous tense, 67
Present tense, changed for indirect speech, 53
Punctuation, 237
    with appositives, 52–53
    with dependent clauses, 11
    with introductory phrases, 50–52
    in a series, 13–14, 208–9

Relative clauses, 250, 267, 268–72, 281–84
    for describing, 250–56
Relative pronoun, omitting, 271–72
Reports. *See* Objective reporting
Restrictive clauses, 268–71, 281–82

Sentences
    active, 218–20
    passive, 218–20. *See also* Irrelevant sentences
Series, punctuation for, 13–14, 208, 221
Should, 15
    using, to give instructions, 10–11, 26
Similarities, 159, 171–72
    finding, 139–43
Similarly, for transition, 178
So, to show cause-effect, 124–26
Specific words, 196, 202–3
Such as, to give examples, 235

Tense
    in active or passive sentences, 218–20
    with indirect speech, 53, 67
    past, 53, 67–69
    past continuous, 67
    present, 53
    present continuous, 67
Terminology, using accurate, 242
That, to introduce a restrictive clause, 269
Therefore, to show cause-effect, 124–26
Then, for chronological order, 32
Transitions, 233–34
    to show additions, 95–96
    to show chronological order, 4–5, 22–23, 32–34
    to show contrast, 147–49, 162, 178–79
    for giving examples, 206–7

Verbs
    imperative form, 6
    to be with comparatives, 151
    to be with relative clauses, 271–72
    See also Tense

When, 11–12, 110–11
Which
    to introduce relative clauses, 250
    to introduce restrictive clauses, 269
Who, to introduce relative clauses, 250
Words, general and specific, 196, 202–3

CORRECTION SYMBOLS

sp	spelling error	Incorrect:	Go ~~too~~ the post office. *(sp)*
		Correct:	Go to the post office.
cap	capitalization error	Incorrect:	I live on ~~main~~ ~~street~~. *(cap cap)*
		Correct:	I live on Main Street.
p	punctuation error	Incorrect:	I ate an egg and toast. *(p)*
		Correct:	I ate an egg and toast.
wd	wrong word	Incorrect:	I ~~have~~ 21 years old. *(wd)*
		Correct:	I am 21 years old.
wf	wrong word form	Incorrect:	He runs ~~slow~~. *(wf)*
		Correct:	He runs slowly.
⌒	connect the letters	Incorrect:	People can̑ot drive in the U.S. without a license.
		Correct:	People cannot drive in the U.S. without a license.
agr	agreement error	Incorrect:	Jalal always arrive late. *(agr)*
		Correct:	Jalal always arrives late.
ref	reference error	Incorrect:	Everybody must do their own work. *(ref)*
		Correct:	Everybody must do his own work.
∧	something is missing here	Incorrect:	They planned to go to restaurant.
		Correct:	They planned to go to a restaurant.
↻→	move word or phrase here	Incorrect:	Sarah at night watches T.V.
		Correct:	Sarah watches T.V. at night.
T	verb tense error	Incorrect:	I go to the movies yesterday. *(T)*
		Correct:	I went to the movies yesterday.

CORRECTION SYMBOLS **299**

frag	sentence fragment	Incorrect:	Khadiza is always tired. (Because she goes to bed late.) *frag*
		Correct:	Khadiza is always tired because she goes to bed late.
run-on	run-on sentence	Incorrect:	Zaida understands English, *run-on* she can't speak it.
		Correct:	Zaida understands English, but she can't speak it.
trans	transition needed	Incorrect:	Pierre did well on his examination. *trans* He failed the course.
		Correct:	Pierre did well on his examination. However, he failed the course.
w trans	wrong transition	Incorrect:	Omar plays tennis. (On the other hand,) *w trans* he plays soccer.
		Correct:	Omar plays tennis. In addition, he plays soccer.
/	separate words	Incorrect:	Turn/on the light.
		Correct:	Turn on the light.
X	omit this	Incorrect:	Dang ⨯he is sick and can't come to class.
		Correct:	Dang is sick and can't come to class.
[?]	not clear		This symbol is used when your instructor does not know what you mean.
¶	new paragraph		This symbol is used when indentation is needed to indicate a new paragraph.
no¶	no new paragraph		This is used to indicate that a new paragraph should not be started here.